Probers Suspect Stuart Killed Wife to Collect
Insurance, Start Restaurant *(Boston Globe)*

MAYOR FLYNN: MY ACTIONS RIGHT IN
STUART CASE *(Boston Herald)*

BLACK LEADERS ASK REVIEW OF
STUART PROBE *(Boston Globe)*

Lawyer Tells Who Knew of Boston Plot *(New
York Newsday)*

PRESUMED INNOCENT: Because Charles
Stuart was white and affluent, he almost got
away with murder. Now Boston must ponder
why it so readily believed his lie. *(Time*
magazine)

"MURDER AND DECEIT": A Cold Killer's
Chilling Charade *(People* magazine)

MURDER IN BOSTON

FROM COAST TO COAST, NEWS OF A STARTLING TRAGEDY

'A TERRIBLE NIGHT': Gunman Invades Car, Shoots Couple (*Boston Herald*)

'HERO' IN WIFE'S DEATH KILLS HIMSELF IN PLUNGE (New York *Daily News*)

KIN BLEW WHISTLE ON KILLER: Kid Brother Went to Boston Cops (New York *Daily News*)

ILLUSION AND TRAGEDY COEXIST AFTER A COUPLE DIES (*The New York Times*)

'Romance' Suspected in Boston Slay (New York *Daily News*)

BOSTON MURDER SUSPECT SOUGHT A BROTHER'S HELP, LAWYER SAYS (*The New York Times*)

Michael: What's going to happen?
Shelly: We're going to tell Mom and Dad.
Michael: What are you going to tell them?
Shelly: We're going to tell them we know that Chuck was involved. We're not going to tell them that he killed her.
Michael: Yeah, right.
Shelly: Okay.
Michael: Wow.
Shelly: I know, Mike. Get ready.

It became apparent that Charles Stuart's terrible crime would soon be revealed. As each shocking clue surfaced, new mysteries emerged—frightening questions that demand answers before the hidden truth about that horrible night on Mission Hill can be revealed fully. Did Charles Stuart—known as "Chuck" to family and friends—actually pull the trigger, or was there in fact a third person who wielded the gun? Did Stuart leap voluntarily from Tobin Bridge to his death in the icy water below? Why have the police and the press been so unwilling to release important information about either the double murder or Stuart's alleged suicide? MURDER IN BOSTON is a relentlessly probing look at a crime that shattered two families—and stunned an entire nation.

MURDER
IN
BOSTON

Ken Englade

ST. MARTIN'S PAPERBACKS

MURDER IN BOSTON

ISBN: 0-312-92396-1

Printed in the United States of America

St. Martin's Paperbacks edition/May 1990

10 9 8 7 6 5 4 3 2 1

For the Yankee branch: Ron, Regina, Alison, and Emily

ACKNOWLEDGMENTS

Without special help from a number of people, this book would not have been possible. The road to publication was not always straight and clearly marked, but when I tended to go off on a secondary trail or got lost in the forest of Boston politics, these people helped me get back on course. Whether I succeeded in staying there has yet to be determined. Nevertheless, I am extremely grateful for their assistance and support. Dr. James Smith stole time from a busy practice to keep me honest. He had the toughest job of all, but he did it well. Similarly, my daughter, Michelle, who should have been studying for her bar exam, used her time instead to perform valuable legal research. I hope her future clients appreciate her work as much as I. Ron and Regina Englade fielded a million of my questions and patiently suffered my ramblings. That is above and beyond the call of family, but they didn't hesitate. Others also helped in a hundred different ways, sometimes when they may not have even realized how much of a service they were performing. They include, but are not limited to, Sergeant Leo Gerstel, Gary McLaughlin, Lieutenant Dave Peterson, Robert Abrams, Mary Travers, Terry Ann Knopf, Cheryl O'Donnell, Tom Janssen, Mark Jurkowitz, and Kevin Convey. And, of course, there is the person who made it all possible: my editor, Charles Spicer. May they all be rich and happy.

AUTHOR'S NOTE

In the late 1800s Roman Catholic authorities in Boston ordered the establishment of a mission to serve poor immigrants who were flowing into the area from Ireland. The mission centered around a church, Our Lady of Perpetual Help, which was built atop an elevation called Parker Hill. The church was consecrated in 1877, and from then on the piece of landscape on which it was built began taking on a new identity. Over the years the name "Parker" was lost and the area became known simply as Mission Hill.

The first pastor of the mission was the Reverend James Healy, the son of an Irishman and a former slave. Healy later became the country's first black Catholic bishop. His mixed-race heritage set the tone for the neighborhood, which now is one of the most diverse in Boston with a population of 45 percent white, 30 percent Hispanic, 20 percent black, and 5 percent Asian. The broad mix, however, does not by any stretch of the imagination insure tranquillity. Healy's ascent to prominence and responsibility proved a poor man from a racial minority could rise above such handicaps. But those were the days before drugs, apathy, street crime, and racial animosity spread throughout the neighborhood like a plague. By the autumn of 1989 Mission Hill had a reputation as a crime-infested ghetto where casual visitors, especially white visitors, were both unwelcome and unsafe. It was an area that many savvy Bostonians regarded with caution. It was a neighborhood through which white motorists drove warily, if at all. While they were in transit, they commonly rolled up their windows and locked their car doors. It was an area where anything could happen and more than likely would. Generally speaking, Bostonians were ready to believe any horror story at all about Mission Hill, particularly if race were a factor. That did not excuse what was to unfold in Mission Hill in the forthcoming days and weeks, but it helped explain why events transpired as they did.

The full story of what happened in Mission Hill has not yet been told. Perhaps it never will be. It is only in fiction that murders are neatly solved and all the loose ends are conveniently tied up. The reader will not find that to be the result in this instance. There are considerably more questions about what *really* happened on the night of October 23, 1989, than there currently are answers. But that in itself is part of the story. In the following pages, I have tried to present all the publicly known facts surrounding the murder of Carol Stuart and the alleged suicide of her husband. In some cases I show where the "facts" do not fit the circum-stances. In other cases I show where there are exceedingly valid questions that remain unan-swered. And they will remain that way until au-thorities are more forthcoming with things they *do* know the answer to, basic things valuable to the resolution of any murder, things like the ballistics report on the pistol pulled from the Pines River, the text of the note found on the seat of Charles Stuart's car, the autopsy reports on Charles and Carol . . . But I'm getting ahead of the story.

The fact that many of these details are not known puts everyone on an equal footing. Every reader can become an armchair detective. Every reader can come to his or her own conclusions. Everyone is entitled to an opinion. I'll give you mine at the other end of the text, but along the way I will show how and why I have come to that point.

This will not be the definitive book on the deaths of Charles and Carol Stuart. It is, in a sense, an interim report designed to offer food for thought as much as to explain. If nothing else, it will show why this is such a complex case and why it is a mystery that will continue to fascinate readers of true crime for years to come.

Ken Englade

Chapter 1

October 23, 1989
Monday
8:10 P.M.

Carol Stuart crawled awkwardly into the Toyota's passenger seat, straining with a frustration familiar to every woman who has ever carried a child. At seven months Carol was obviously pregnant and feeling more bloated by the hour. Even everyday tasks, like putting on her shoes and getting in and out of a car, were becoming more strenuous, more aggravating. It was a burden, but it would soon be over, she reminded herself, and then it would have all been worth it. Her delivery would not only be a personal relief, but it would be the most wonderful gift she could give her husband, Chuck, both for Christmas and his birthday, which was one week earlier. Let it be a boy, she had been praying ever since she'd got confirmation from her doctor, a son to make Chuck happy. He loved children, she knew, because he spent hours working with them in his old neighborhood, refereeing their basketball games and coaching the Little Leaguers. Chuck himself had been through the programs, playing both baseball and basketball. Now, nearing thirty, he wanted to give something back, to help other clumsy youngsters as he himself had been helped. Soon, she hoped, he would have one more boy to coach: his own son. And one of the most wonderful things about her first pregnancy, Carol thought, smiling inwardly, was the timing. What better time could a good Catholic girl from a devout Italian family have picked to have a child than at Christmas?

These thoughts cheered her, made her feel less like a bandy-legged behemoth. But then the depression intruded again. As she struggled to stretch the seat belt across her distended abdomen, she wondered how many more times she was going to have to lengthen the strap to accommodate her growing bulk. But the concept was fleeting. A happy, cheerful person by nature, Carol seldom dwelt on negatives. All her life she had been a bubbly, extroverted person, one who invariably saw the good side of everything, especially people. Carol always had something nice to say about everyone, no matter how aggravating an individual appeared to others. It was a wonderful trait to possess in an increasingly cynical world, and it represented her true beauty. A pretty enough girl with long dark hair and flashing brown eyes, she could nevertheless hardly be regarded as glamorous. Her mouth was too wide, her nose a little too prominent, for her ever to be considered as a magazine cover girl. But her loveliness came from within. When she smiled, two rows of startlingly white teeth shone like a beacon to her soul. It was almost impossible for anyone to talk to Carol for more than five minutes and not come away feeling refreshed. She was intuitive about others' problems, seeming to know by instinct what to say and how to soothe. This in itself was a reflection of her intelligence, a mirroring of her ability to reason and understand—and the desire to want to—that made her a top student through high school and won her membership in the prestigious National Honor Society. At Boston College, a respected Catholic university only fifteen miles from her parents' home in suburban Medford, her grades put her near the top of her class. After she earned her undergraduate degree in political science, having early on abandoned the desire to follow her older brother into education and be, like him, a high school teacher, she enrolled almost immediately in the law school at Suffolk University, a Boston institution popular with fledgling politicians. With her J.D. degree and bar passage certificate in hand, she knocked on the door of a local publishing company and was immediately hired to work as a tax attorney. But at age thirty, a few months older than her husband, she began to think more about a family than a career. It was time to have a baby, she decided.

As she reached across to fit the buckle of the seat belt into the bracket between the front seats, her hand brushed an instrument resting silently in its cradle: a car phone, a present from Chuck the previous April to celebrate her first month of pregnancy. The blue Cressida was *her* car, and Chuck had said he wanted her to have the phone as added protection on her journeys through the city. Boston, like any metropolis, had its good areas and its bad ones, the safe parts sometimes blending without warning into the unsafe ones. It was possible to be driving one minute through a perfectly respectable, gentrified, yuppified neighborhood like the South End, and then, without benefit of notice, be traveling a minute later through a mean-streeted district of grim housing projects and rowdy bars. Here crack cocaine passed from hand to hand as a matter of ordinary commerce and addicts, desperate to find a way to finance their next fix, were all too eager to relieve naive interlopers of whatever cash or negotiable items they might have been foolish enough to tote with them.

Take the place they were in right then: the parking garage attached to one of the country's best-known health care facilities, Brigham and Women's Hospital. Carol and Chuck had been in the hospital to attend a birthing class. It was a famous and respected maternity hospital, and neither Carol nor Chuck wanted anything but the best. After all, they could afford it. Carol was making some $40,000 a year in her job, and Chuck, the general manager at the city's most respected independent furriers, Edward F. Kakas & Sons, located on tony Newbury Street, drew a salary of $103,000 a year. Plus, there was his annual bonus, which sometimes went as high as $35,000. In a good year the two of them could pull in more than $175,000, which wasn't at all bad for a young couple just starting out. It was not unreasonable for them to want the most attentive care possible for Carol.

Unhappily, though, Brigham and Women's was not located in one of the city's stellar neighborhoods, situated as it was on the fringe of Roxbury. A once fashionable section populated by the city's elite, Roxbury had, over the years, gradually eroded. Historian Theodore White, in his autobiographical tome *In Search of History*, recalls Roxbury when he was growing up nearby in the 1920s as a declining neighborhood that shortly before had been home to the city's prosperous shoe factories. But the factories closed during the Great Depression, and the neighborhood went farther downhill. As is common in large cities, the older inner neighborhoods were abandoned by their original inhabitants, who fled to the suburbs. Their old dwellings were taken over by poorer residents, the newer immigrants. In Roxbury, particularly Mission Hill, this meant first the Irish, then blacks and Orientals. In the spring of 1968, after the assassination of Dr. Martin Luther King, Jr., in Memphis, blacks across the country rioted in their ghettos. In Boston the ghetto was Roxbury. Since then an uneasy peace, more like a truce, had settled over the area, but the currents of racial tension flowed strongly just below the surface. There was a lot of black/white antagonism in Boston, and much of it was rooted in Roxbury.

Although Roxbory proper is a little southeast of Brigham and Women's Hospital, the distance is not great. One thing many outsiders fail to realize about Boston is how small, how compact, the city actually is. Boston itself covers only 45.5 square miles, and its population is slightly under 500,000. Of this total, some 85,000 people, roughly 17 percent of the total, are black. The millions of people most think of as Bostonians are actually residents of the small communities that surround the city, bedroom communities like Lexington, Woburn, Quincy, Framingham, Groton, Revere, Medford, and Reading. Carol, in fact, grew up in Medford; Chuck in Revere. They currently lived in Reading, in a luxurious $239,000 home complete with a heated swimming pool in the backyard. But, like many others, they made their living in Boston and depended on the city for its facilities, like health care.

The neighborhood around Brigham and Women's can best be described as "mixed," mixed racially, culturally, and by class. On one side is Roxbury, another Mission Hill, and throughout are peppered some of the city's most distinguished institutions. Within a comfortable walk from where Carol and Chuck were getting into their Toyota was Northeastern University, the Museum of Fine Arts, Boston Latin High School (whose alumni include Theodore White), Beth Israel Hospital, Peter Brent Brigham Hospital, Harvard Medical School, and the Massachusetts College of Pharmacy, all of which have outstanding reputations in their respected fields. But despite the proximity of these celebrated institutions, the neighborhood was still regarded as an extremely dangerous one. It was, in fact, one of the city's premier high-crime spots. To the Boston police department, it is part of Area B, a 1.5-square-mile chunk that includes Roxbury, Mattapan, and part of Dorchester. From a criminologist's point of view, there is little comforting, intellectual, or healthful about Area B. In a forty-day period ending the previous week, there were 170 reported shootings in the district, an average of 4.25 per day. So far that year there had been seventy-seven murders in all of Boston, but more than half of them were in Area B, which is one of five districts the police use to subdivide the city. By the end of the year, one hundred murders were recorded in the city, fifty-five of them in Area B.

Neither Chuck nor Carol was ignorant of these statistics. Before he left work that afternoon to meet Carol, Chuck and a co-worker, Peter Jaworski, had talked about the dangerous neighborhood in which Brigham and Women's was located. As Chuck walked out the door onto Newbury Street, which was jammed as usual with upscale shoppers, Jaworski gave him a piece of advice: "Be careful," he said.

While Carol had some difficulty slipping into the Toyota because of her pregnancy, her husband had problems for a different reason. A husky, avid sportsman who kept fit with basketball and weight lifting when he could steal the time from his job and his wife, Chuck was not suited physically to the conflicting dimensions of a Japanese import; his legs were too long and his shoulders too broad for him to get comfortable. That may have been one reason he didn't own a car of his own. The Toyota was Carol's car *and* the family car. If he needed transportation, he usually borrowed his employer's van, which was considerably more commodious. But this was a personal errand, and he elected to drive the Toyota rather than take the Kakas vehicle. Scrunching behind the wheel, he fastened his seat belt and started the engine.

If the two made small talk, they may have commented on the beautiful weather they were enjoying. Although autumn is almost always a glorious season in Massachusetts, 1989 was particularly nice. Traditionally autumn is when the New England foliage takes on magnificent hues of gold and scarlet, and there is enough nip in the air to set the blood coursing wildly through summer-numbed veins. Bodies that have been lethargic through July, August, and part of September are miraculously rejuvenated when the nights turn chilly and the chlorophyll disappears from the oaks and elms. A New England autumn is one of the wonders of the American world, and each year thousands come from all points on the compass to revel in the splendor. This year the fall had been a particularly splendid one. In mid-October Indian summer made a welcome visit and surprised and delighted everyone by settling in for a prolonged stay. The sky turned a remarkable blue; the Charles River glowed with a penetrating incandescence. The sun shined brightly; the grass held its brilliant summer green, and the trees glowed as radiantly as if they had been touched by a modern Midas. It was a wonderful time to be alive. For Carol, that would be the final irony.

Maneuvering out of the hospital, Chuck came out on Francis Street, a narrow thoroughfare running northwest-southeast between Huntington and Brookline Avenues. Chuck's expected action would have been to turn right, toward Reading. Instead he turned left, toward Huntington, into the heart of Mission Hill. Carol, perhaps preoccupied with what she had learned in that evening's Lamaze class or reveling in the mild night, may not have noticed. Even if she had, it would not have made much difference. The decision was made. In roughly twenty minutes, about the time it takes to drink a sociable cup of coffee, Carol would be effectively dead.

Chapter 2

October 23, 1989
8:35 P.M.

In the late 1980s, when car telephones began proliferating at a near astronomical rate, Massachusetts law enforcement officials set up a special computer network to handle emergency calls from motorists. Although there are two other ways of dialing the Massachusetts State Police from cellular telephones—either through 1-800-525-5555 or, much more simply, *77—the emergency dialing number of choice across the country is 911. Planners figured that when dialing for help, motorists would not differentiate between a cellular phone and a regular phone, so they factored the 911 code into the system. In Boston, a regular phone user dialing 911 is connected to the Boston Police Department Communications Center area, also known as "the turret." But a motorist dialing 911 from his car is switched via computer to the Massachusetts State Police Communications Center, called "the bunker," which is housed in a twenty-foot-by-thirty-foot cavelike room buried in a drab, featureless building at 1010 Commonwealth Avenue, not far from Boston University.

Depending on the day (the weekends are far busier), the bunker is manned by one to three civilian dispatchers and a state trooper who acts as shift commander. The calls are handled by the civilians. The trooper is there in case law enforcement authority is necessary, since the state police have responsibility for investigating all felony crimes anywhere in Massachusetts except in Boston proper, where they are handled by the city police. In any given month the dispatchers field 250 to 300 calls a day; the heaviest periods are weekend nights. Monday nights are generally fairly slow. Experience has shown that dispatchers working the evening trick on a Monday will receive about seventy-five calls between three and eleven P.M., which is enough of a workload to keep two people busy, but not enough to justify having a third person on duty. On Monday, October 23, dispatchers Gary McLaughlin and Jack Moran were manning the desk, which runs down the center of the room and is flanked by stacks of metal boxes jammed with electronic gear. The trooper acting as shift commander, seated at a desk in a small alcove at the rear of the room, was Sergeant Daniel Grabowski. Among them, the men have some sixty years' experience in law enforcement work.

McLaughlin, a shy, graying thirty-five-year-old who signed on with the state police at the end of his freshman year at Boston State College, was taking a quick breather after a particularly harrowing call involving an attempted murder on the western edge of their territory. His pulse was just returning to normal when the phone at his elbow shrilled insistently.

"State police, Boston," McLaughlin answered, hoping to hear an angry motorist complaining about a reckless driver or a Good Samaritan reporting a fender bender. What he got was another crisis. Over the line came the unmistakable sound of tortured breathing: a wheeze, a grunt, a disembodied sound sending an immediate chill down McLaughlin's spine. Then a male voice sobbed, "My wife's been shot. I've been shot."

McLaughlin's pulse rate soared. "Where is this, sir?" he asked briskly.

"I have no idea," the voice replied, heavy with pain.

"Try to give me an indication of where you might be," McLaughlin pressed, "a cross street, anything."

There was a long silence. "Hello?" the voice said, sounding fainter.

"Yes, go ahead," McLaughlin replied, exchanging a significant glance with Moran, who was seated at the main communications console some three feet away. Without a word, both Moran and Grabowski reached for their phones and plugged into McLaughlin's line. The call, like all others that come in through the network, was being recorded, but McLaughlin, Grabowski, and Moran acted as a tight-knit team. When there was an emergency they all pitched in to help. As McLaughlin hunched over the desk, the voice of the caller fed through three receivers.

"He got into the car at Huntington Avenue," the voice said. "I drove straight through Huntington Avenue."

"Where are you right now, sir?" McLaughlin urged. "Can you indicate to me?"

"No," the voice said, beginning to sound panicky. "I don't know. He drove us . . . he made us go to an abandoned area."

One of the disadvantages of having all 911 calls from cellular phones switched automatically to the bunker was that dispatchers have no idea where the call may be coming from until they are told by the caller. They could be anywhere in Greater Boston, anywhere within reach of the giant state police antenna. But as soon as the caller said Huntington Avenue, McLaughlin knew he was in Boston proper. So did Grabowski, who was already grabbing another phone and dialing through to Boston PD on a separate line. He wanted to get the city police active as soon as possible. Independent of the trooper's action, Moran swung into action on the city police's emergency radio channel.

"Okay," McLaughlin said as soothingly as he could. "Can you see out the windows? Can you tell me where you are?"

There was a pause. "No, I don't know," the man replied. "I don't see any signs." He groaned, "Oh, God."

"What kind of car do you have?" McLaughlin asked.

"Toyota Cressida," the man replied immediately.

"You're in the city of Boston, though?" Mc-

Laughlin asked, determined to confirm his suspicions.

"Yes," the voice said.

"Can you give me any indications where you might be, any buildings?"

The man groaned heavily. "No," he croaked.

"Okay," McLaughlin said calmly, deciding to take another tack. The important thing, he felt, was to keep the communication going, keep the line open. "Has your wife been shot as well?"

"Yes," the voice replied. "In the head."

McLaughlin grimaced. "Okay," he said, trying to keep emotion out of his voice. "Bear with me now. Stand by. Stay on the phone with me."

"Should I try to drive?"

"No," McLaughlin answered quickly. "The people that shot you, are they in the area right there?"

"No," the voice replied. "They took off. They left."

"Okay," McLaughlin directed. "Can you look out? Can you get out of the vehicle and look around to see where you are, sir? I'm trying to get some assistance to you."

Boston PD, tipped by the street name, was already rushing cars to the area. They got another clue when the caller said he and his wife had just left Brigham and Women's Hospital when the attack occurred. Since he said he had not gone far, that meant he probably was in Roxbury. It was not a great area in which to lie wounded and helpless.

"Should I drive up to the corner of the street?" the man asked, a touch of panic seeming to creep into his voice.

McLaughlin considered that briefly. "If you can

drive without hurting yourself, yes," he replied. But he felt intuitively that it would be better if the police could find him before he moved. "Just try to give me a cross street," McLaughlin repeated patiently. "If you can drive, give me any street indication, and stay there. I'll get someone right to you."

"I'll start the car," the man said weakly. "He took the keys, but I have a spare set." He groaned loudly. "Oh, man." Then he spoke again: "I'm starting the car."

"Okay," McLaughlin said, adding almost off-handedly, "What's your name, sir?"

"Stuart," the man moaned. "Chuck Stuart." The effort of giving his name seemed to be immense. He stuttered painfully, "Ahhh, man."

"Bear with me, Chuck," McLaughlin said as encouragingly as he could. "I'm going to get someone to you. Hang in with me, now."

While McLaughlin and Chuck were talking, Boston police cars were crisscrossing the area, trying to locate a single stopped car among thousands.

In the meantime, Chuck had started to move. "I'm at a place," he mumbled into the phone. "But I can't read it."

"Just try to read it, Chuck," McLaughlin urged. "Just calm down. Just stay with me. I'm going to get help to you. Help is on the way."

"I'm coming up to an intersection, but there's no—"

"What color is your car, buddy?" McLaughlin interrupted.

"Blue."

"Blue Toyota Cressida?" McLaughlin said, wanting to be sure.

"Yeah," Chuck confirmed.

"Okay, Chuck, help is on the way. Bear with me. Is your wife breathing?"

There was a slight pause. "She's still gurgling," Chuck replied. Another pause. "There's a busy street up ahead, but I can't see where I am."

"Hang in with me, Chuck," McLaughlin urged again. "Just try to give me any indication of where you might be. Can you see a building?"

"I'm driving with my lights off," Chuck replied. "I can't reach forward. It's too painful."

"Just tell me what the street is, Chuck."

"Ahhh, man!" Chuck screamed. "I'm pulling over." Then, almost in a whisper, "Tremont Street."

"You're at Tremont?" McLaughlin asked excitedly.

Chuck apparently did not register the question. "Oh, man," he groaned. "I'm going to pass out, and my wife has stopped gurgling. She's stopped breathing. I'm going to try to drive straight to the hospital."

"Can you drive?" McLaughlin asked insistently.

"I'm trying."

"Chuck," McLaughlin said authoritatively, "pull over to the side of the street and talk to any passerby so I have an indication of where you are."

"I can't move," Chuck replied, his voice rising. "Oh, God."

"Chuck," McLaughlin said tensely, "can you see anyone on the street?"

"My car died," Chuck replied. "Oh, man."

"Chuck," McLaughlin said urgently. "Chuck. Can you see anything? . . . Chuck? . . . Chuck?" Then, faintly through the phone, he heard a familiar sound in the background. "Do you hear a siren?"

"Yes," Chuck said softly. "I can hear a siren."

Grabowski and Moran had already focused on the siren. Speaking though Boston PD, they asked the patrol car drivers, one at a time, to turn on their sirens as they wound through the neighborhood's dark, narrow, twisting streets. Everyone in the bunker could hear the sirens over the three-way connection. By having the drivers activate their sirens in sequence, they could tell which patrol cars were closer to the Stuart vehicle and which ones were moving away. It was, in essence, a deadly serious game of blindman's buff. Going strictly by sound, Grabowski and Moran directed the police cars ever nearer to the scene.

"Can you hear me, Chuck?" McLaughlin urged. "Chuck, pick up the phone. I can hear you breathing there, Chuck. Come on, buddy."

"I hear the police," Chuck said, relief evident in his voice. "Right here," he said. "There's Boston police."

In the background McLaughlin could hear a third voice. "We've located him," it said.

Then he heard Chuck one more time. "Get my wife out," he heard him say.

It took about fifteen minutes from the time McLaughlin answered the phone for rescuers to find Chuck and Carol. At 8:50 P.M., a patrol car driven by Officer Wayne Rock braked to a halt beside a blue Toyota, which was pulled to the side of the road on St. Alphonsus Street near Horadan Way, a broad alley that plunged darkly into a dismal housing project. Rock flung open his door and dashed to the Toyota. He took one quick look and gasped, his eyes focused on Carol Stuart's bulging stomach. Turning to his partner, he sobbed, "Oh, Jesus Christ, she's pregnant." It was a sight he would not quickly forget. The vision of a hugely pregnant woman with a bullet in her head would haunt him for a long time.

Seconds later an ambulance roared up, and the fight began to save Carol's and Chuck's lives. Attendants turned first to Carol, who was slumped in the passenger seat, her chin on her chest and her head tilted inward, toward the center of the car. Gently they extricated her, laid her carefully on a gurney, and rolled her to the ambulance for the short trip back to Brigham and Women's Hospital.

9:12 P.M.

Surgeons at Brigham and Women's took one look at Carol as she was wheeled into the emergency room and rushed her straight into surgery. Her wound was about as bad as it could be. The bullet had entered the left side of the back of her head, and there was extensive brain damage. She was barely alive. One of the first decisions doctors made was to remove Carol's child by cesarean section. The baby was a boy, as Carol had hoped. He weighed only three pounds, and doctors feared his death was imminent. Soon after he was taken from Carol, a priest was called and a brief Catholic baptismal ceremony was held in the intensive care unit. The baby was christened Christopher, which was the name Chuck and Carol had decided upon.

Carol, meanwhile, was kept alive by technology. But it was a futile battle. A few hours later, at three A.M. on Tuesday, October 24, some six and a half hours after she was shot, Carol died without ever regaining consciousness. Whether there was a decision by family members and physicians to discontinue life support or whether she died in spite of the surgeons' best efforts is not known. Physicians at Brigham and Women's never described Carol's wound in detail, and authorities did not release an autopsy report.

Chuck was wheeled into a separate ambulance, and instead of Brigham and Women's, he was rushed to Boston City Hospital. En route, a paramedic skillfully ran his hands over Chuck's chest and abdomen. "Just one wound," he told a colleague. "An entry in the side, but no exit." The slug, a chunk of lead a little larger than a pencil eraser, was still in Chuck's gut. During the ride, Chuck faded in and out of consciousness, but even when he was awake he was mainly silent. When he did talk it was to ask about the seriousness of his wound and to inquire, perceptively enough, if he would have to wear a colostomy bag. The paramedics who made the journey with him would later reflect upon his behavior and would, in retrospect, claim they found it peculiar that he never asked about his wife.

At BCH Chuck also was taken straight into surgery. As in Carol's case, officials at BCH never gave

more than a superficial description of Chuck's
wounds, saying only that he suffered damage to his
liver, urological tract, stomach, and intestines.
Some major blood vessels were said to be damaged
or severed. But even without the details there was
no doubt that doctors considered Chuck's injuries
to be extremely serious; Chuck came very close to
death himself. A few days after the initial operation
he had to undergo surgery again. All told, he spent
five weeks in intensive care and he lost fifty pounds.
At no time, said the doctor who performed the
surgery, did anyone suspect that the wound was
self-inflicted.

Chuck's injuries were psychological as well as
physical. When he awoke hours later he had to be
told that his wife was dead. Their baby, a boy, had
survived, he was told, although he was fighting for
his life. Having absorbed that news, Chuck had to
accept one more blow. Peeking beneath the sheets,
he discovered that his worst fear had come true:
firmly attached to his abdomen with stubborn ad-
hesive was a small plastic bag. His intestines were
so badly ripped by the bullet that the colon had
had to be sealed off temporarily and left to repair
on its own, a surgical procedure called a colostomy.
Chuck would have to wear bags for two or three
months, changing them at least once a day.

Chapter 3

According to firearms experts, a .38-caliber slug fired into a human body is not likely, under normal circumstances, to go completely through the person. Although the slug leaves the barrel traveling at about 850 feet per second, human tissue is dense enough to slow it down quickly. This was especially true in the Stuart shooting because authorities later determined that the ammunition in the pistol that fired the shots was ten years old, and by then the gunpowder had started to lose a lot of its power. The fact that neither of the bullets went through the bodies was not something that drew investigators' attention. They were far more interested in what Chuck had to say than they were in ballistics. And Chuck had plenty to say. As soon as he was conscious enough to talk, he gave detectives an account of what happened that shocked police, politicians, and much of the public.

He and Carol had no sooner left the hospital, he said, than they had to stop for a traffic light at Brigham Circle. While waiting for the light to change, a black man armed with a "silver" pistol forced his way into their Toyota and announced he intended to rob them.

"Turn left here and then drive straight ahead," he said in a raspy, singsong voice, slipping into the backseat. Then he added: "And don't look in the rearview mirror."

Chuck wheeled left onto Tremont Street and drove for several blocks, toward the Roxbury Crossing subway station, a major stop on the Orange Line. Just before they got to the T station, the gunman ordered Chuck to turn right, into a dark, lonely block conspicuous by its abundance of vacant lots. A few hundred yards farther on was the sprawling Bromley-Heath housing project, a crime-ridden neighborhood regarded by most white residents of Boston as a no-man's-land.

"Pull over," the gunman growled, gesturing to a deserted corner. When Chuck stopped the car, the gunman demanded first the car keys and then their money and jewelry. They were terrified, Chuck told police, and hastened to comply. As Chuck yanked the keys out of the ignition and handed them to the man, Carol passed over her blue-and-tan Gucci handbag, which contained her wallet stuffed with about $100 in cash; her dinner ring, which was made up of a marquise ruby surrounded by small diamonds; and her engagement ring, a raised 1.5-carat solitaire on a yellow gold band. When the

gunman turned to Chuck, he handed over his gold
Seiko LaSalle quartz watch with its gold band.

At that point, Chuck said, things suddenly went
to hell. When the gunman demanded Chuck's wallet as well and Chuck said he didn't carry one, the
man looked incredulous. He glanced down at the
car phone, and a look of rage swept over his face.
Apparently, investigators theorized, the man figured Chuck didn't want to hand him his wallet
because it contained a policeman's badge, a suspicion that was substantiated in part by the presence
of the car phone. "You're five-oh!" he screamed,
using the street slang term for police. With that, he
opened fire.

Within the next few seconds, Chuck said, the
gunman shot Carol in the head and fired at Chuck's
head but missed because Chuck ducked at the last
moment. Angry, the man leaned over the seat and
pumped a bullet into Chuck's side, then tried to
shoot him again, but the hammer clicked on an
empty chamber. Without another word, the man
flung open the back door, leaped out of the car, and
ran off into the darkness, taking his booty with
him.

In great pain, Chuck said, he dug an extra set of
car keys out of his pocket since Carol's had been in
the ignition, started the car, and drove away seeking help. It was then, he said, that he called the
state police and got dispatcher Gary McLaughlin.

Despite the gunman's admonition not to look at
him, Chuck was able to give police a remarkably
detailed description of the assailant. He was a
brown-skinned, brown-eyed man between twenty-
eight and thirty-four years old, five feet ten inches

tall, and thin, weighing only 150 to 160 pounds, Chuck said. He also had high cheekbones, a bony jaw that was covered with a patchy beard, a "medium Nubian" nose, and he wore his hair in a short afro. His most distinguishing physical characteristic, Chuck said, was his voice. As for clothing, the man was wearing a dark shirt covered by a black sweatsuit. The sweatsuit jacket had two or three red stripes on the sleeve. He also had on a black baseball-style hat and black driving gloves with the knuckles cut out. He was right-handed, Chuck added, and he seemed especially nervous.

Considering the short time the man was in the car and the fact that he was not directly in Chuck's line of sight, the description was incredibly detailed. But at the time no one thought it strange, least of all, apparently, the police.

Since the incident occurred rather late in the evening, the story broke too late to make much of a splash in the next morning's papers. Despite the late break, however, the *Boston Globe* carried a brief piece on its front page on October 24. Headlined COUPLE SHOT AFTER LEAVING HOSPITAL; BABY DELIVERED, the two-column piece by *Globe* staffers Peter S. Canellos and Irene Serge gave the bare bones of what had happened even though some of the initial facts were garbled. It gave Carol's age, for example, as thirty-three instead of thirty, and it said she was between five and seven months pregnant. But most of the other details were right on target. What was remarkable about the story, which after a few paragraphs below the fold on page one was continued well to the back of the paper, on page 79, was how it zeroed in immediately on the dramatic exchange over the car phone and the political implications. Reporters Canellos and Serge managed to get several quotes from dispatcher McLaughlin, who told them how unusual it was to receive such a call and how fortuitous it was that Chuck and Carol had a cellular phone in their car. "It was a unique call," the *Globe* quoted McLaughlin as saying. "You don't get many of these in your career."

Newspaper editors do not get many local stories with such potential for drama during their careers, either, and the Boston newspapers moved from the beginning to make the best of the situation. Remarkably, so did public officials. According to the *Globe*, Mayor Raymond Flynn and his hand-picked top cop, Police Commissioner Francis "Mickey" Roache, went immediately to both hospitals to meet with members of Carol's and Chuck's families. Flynn, a dynamic politician with undisguised aspirations to be governor, was notified at home when the incident occurred, and when he showed up to commiserate with the families, he was still clad in a sweatsuit. Sweatsuits seemed to be *the* item for leisure wear in Boston, favored by representatives of all classes.

At a hastily called news conference at a police substation in Roxbury, Flynn promised that he and Roache, a veteran cop with a reputation for competency despite the fact that he had his present job because he was a boyhood friend of the mayor's, would do all they could to apprehend the Stuarts' attacker. "I demand that the Boston Police Department continue to be extremely aggressive in cracking down on people who are using guns and killing innocent people," Flynn said in a prepared statement. "It [the crime situation] is intolerable. We will use every lawful tool to support our police officers in cracking down on gun-wielding criminals."

At this point it is unknown how much of a description of the attacker Chuck had provided to police and how much Flynn knew about what Chuck had said. Given the fact that Chuck was wheeled directly into surgery and was almost certainly still under anesthesia when Flynn met with reporters, neither the officials nor the police had much more to go on than what Chuck had told McLaughlin or perhaps had mumbled to the paramedics en route to BCH. But Flynn did not make his remarks regarding the attack on Chuck and Carol because it was an isolated incident. Although no one would point out until much later that crime in Mission Hill was actually *down* 18 percent in 1989, the public—and probably official—perception was that the neighborhood was a hotbed of criminal activity. In truth this perception was not totally undeserved, not only for Mission Hill, but for Boston as a whole. Carol's murder was number seventy-eight in the city so far that year. At another spot in Mission Hill, not far from where Chuck said he and his wife were shot, a young mother of five had been killed during the summer by a gunshot to the back of her head. It was another apparently random crime, and despite several months of investigation, no one had yet been charged with the murder.

But Mission Hill was not the only neighborhood in Boston with a crime problem. For months police had been fighting drugs and related crimes in other areas. Figuring that drastic circumstances required drastic countermeasures, Boston police instituted a "stop and search" program under which suspicious persons—mainly black youths—could be halted as they transited the city and ordered to prove they were not carrying drugs or firearms. The policy, which had better than lukewarm support among a number of black leaders, would soon be extended to Mission Hill. In the meantime, though, the media was only warming up.

October 25, 1989

The saga of Chuck and Carol built steam rapidly. Because of the time break, the incident received comparatively little press on the first day after it occurred. But by the second day news reports were flying in all directions. Besides being one hell of a story, there were two things that catapulted it from a local-interest item to one that would grip readers and viewers around the world. First, there was the dramatic conversation between Chuck and McLaughlin. By the second day state police had decided to release a copy of the tape of the phone call. As a result, excerpts were blared in broadcast news reports and transcripts were printed in most major newspapers. Second, equally dramatic film had been taken when police and paramedics arrived at the scene. By chance, a camera crew from the television program *Rescue 911* had been riding

with a Boston paramedic team on the night of
October 23. That team was the one that responded
to Chuck's plea for help. When the paramedics
arrived to try to save Chuck's and Carol's lives,
their efforts were performed under the glare of TV
lights. Snippets of the film were aired on the CBS
national news on the night of October 24, and from
there the story took on a life of its own.

By October 25 the Boston newspapers had
jumped on the story with alacrity. It was the lead
story in both the *Globe* and the competing newspaper, the *Boston Herald*, a mildly sensationalist tabloid owned by Australian media magnate Rupert
Murdoch, who also owns *San Antonio Express-News*
and used to own *The New York Post*. In the Wednesday morning *Globe*, the Stuart incident held the
top page one spot, and the spin the editors gave it
would set the tone of media coverage around the
world for the next several months.

READING WOMAN DIES AFTER SHOOTING IN CAR, ran
the main headline, which filled the top quarter of
the page. Under that there was a 1987 photo of a
happy Chuck and Carol, a current photograph of
police officers searching an overgrown lot for the
gun used in the shooting, and two stories. One of
the stories, a featurish semitearjerker by staff
writer Sally Jacobs, who later would write more
narrowly focused profiles, carried the soap-operaish
subhead "The Shattering of a Shining Life."
The other, a more straightforward factual piece,
was headlined simply: HUSBAND, BABY TERMED
CRITICAL. The message in both stories was not subtle: media coverage would take the tack that Chuck
and Carol were a perfect suburban couple who

stumbled into an urban jungle and fell victim to a drug-crazed or drug-hungry black man. Both stories also reflected the barely subdued hysteria that would grip the city in the wake of the incident.

The news piece in one paragraph quoted Police Superintendent Joseph V. Saia, Jr., as saying that there were no leads, but the next paragraph told about how two dozen police officers "raced" to Roxbury to check out a report of two men being seen with a handgun. In that neighborhood, if one were to believe the media, being seen walking the street with a pistol was only one degree more serious than strolling with a bag of groceries.

For the first time, the stories also gave details of Chuck's version of the shootings, and a staff graphic artist whipped out a map showing the pertinent locations on Chuck's and Carol's travels as hostages. They also followed the rough outline established in the previous day's story: that the shooting of Chuck and Carol was not only a crime story, but a political one as well. A third angle, which would not be fully developed until much later, would be the racial implications inherent in the shooting and the investigation.

By the fourth paragraph of the main story, the *Globe* had notified its readers that Chuck and Carol's attack superseded the basics and jumped to the larger issue of crime throughout the city. The fifth paragraph quoted Mayor Flynn, who by then had called for the assignment of "all available detectives" to the case. Presumably, although it was not articulated by reporters Peter J. Howe and Jerry Thomas whose bylines were on the piece, Flynn's call would be made to his old friend Mickey

Roache, who could hardly refuse since he served at Flynn's pleasure.

The next paragraph quoted City Councilor Bruce C. Bolling, a black man who later sided with police opponents, as saying that the Stuart family was "a symbol" of inner-city violence. And the next paragraph, still before the story delved into the details of the incident, quoted Republican party leaders who planned to use the Stuart shooting as a vehicle to push for reinstatement of the death penalty in the state.

The GOP demand was too much even for Flynn, who was quoted in a small boxed story at the bottom of page sixteen as angrily accusing the Republicans of trying to use the incident for "political gain." Needless to say, Flynn is a Democrat.

Both stories were continued—"jumped," in newspaper lingo—in the middle of the paper, where they took up an entire page.

Although it was buried deep in the main story, the issues, perhaps inseparable, of race and class made a tentative early appearance. City Councilor David Scondras, a white man whose district includes Mission Hill, raised the issue almost immediately. Scondras, who also is gay and an outspoken advocate of homosexual rights, cautioned reporters to keep an eye on the race/class angle in their coverage. "You can't help but wonder," he was quoted in the *Globe* as saying, "if what you're watching is a class situation, that it's all right for the poor to put up with an enormous amount of shootings and killings, but, presumably, if you're white, upper-income, and suburban, maybe that changes things."

The possibility that the Stuart case was getting more police attention than other crimes was hinted at even more strongly in a Flynn news conference. A reporter asked Flynn if he saw any irony in the fact that virtually the whole police department was being mobilized to track a black man who had assaulted a white couple while similar efforts had not been made to find assailants of blacks. Nonplussed, Flynn replied: "There will be the same aggressive and fair and consistent enforcement of all our laws, regardless of where it takes place. . . . Whatever area or color or ethnicity, it will be handled in the same aggressive and fair way by the Boston Police Department." The words would later come back to haunt the mayor.

A former college basketball star and, in middle age, an enthusiastic marathon runner, Flynn enjoyed a good reputation, for a white politician, among the city's blacks. Although he had vigorously opposed a busing program that accompanied a school desegregation plan a dozen years previously, Flynn had, as mayor, won over many blacks by his promises to make his administration a more multiracial one than was customary among Boston's elected leaders. He had dramatically increased the number of minorities both in his office and other City Hall departments; he had set aside a disproportionate amount of funds to create lower-priced housing in Roxbury; and he'd pushed Boston banks to make more home mortgage loans available to minorities. In his 1987 bid for reelection, he won in a walk, capturing twenty of twenty-two city wards. The only two he lost were in South Boston, which was his home turf. He lost those because he had been forced by federal pressure to desegregate public housing there. Some of his biggest margins that year were won in black precincts.

But by 1989 he had some problems. Minority spokesmen were critical of him because they did not like his choice of executive director of the Fair Housing Commission, and his requested referendum for an appointed school board was rejected in black neighborhoods. Some also were critical of his obvious pro–law enforcement stance.

So far under his administration, the police department budget had grown by 64 percent, which was well ahead of most other departments. He had also increased the number of police officers by 14 percent, from 1,753 officers to more than 2,000. And he put himself on the front lines. He went on patrol with police in Roxbury; he was prone to show up at hospitals to visit crime victims (the Stuart shooting was not the first time he had dashed out to console a casualty); and, in one memorable confrontation, he stood up to an armed man and his pit bulls.

It was ironic that Flynn, an Irishman, was being called upon to defend himself on charges of discrimination, however tentative they might so far be; not so many years ago the Irish, not the blacks, had been the targets of bigots. But gradually the Irish had moved into positions of power, and now they had a virtual lock on the top political jobs. Witness the Kennedys, former House Speaker Tip O'Neill, and District Attorney Newman Flanagan, to mention but a few. But Flynn is not a run-of-the-mill Irish politician. Although a Democrat, he has never been considered a member of the old party.

In Massachusetts there are three main factions among Democrats: the liberal wing, exemplified by Governor Michael Dukakis (as a Greek, another minority member); the old-line group, of which District Attorney Flanagan is an example; and the maverick faction, which Flynn represents.

Politics is pervasive in Massachusetts, perhaps more than in many other states, so the fact that the story was developing along both criminal and political lines was not surprising. In fact, it would have been shocking if it progressed in any other fashion.

The other, not-so-subtle slant given to the story by the *Globe* was the way Carol and Chuck, and their relationship, were described in almost embarrassing superlatives. Eventually Sally Jacobs and the *Globe* would all but canonize Carol. By then, though, it was determined that Chuck had feet of clay, and a lengthy profile on him was far from favorable. At the beginning, however, there was no hint that they were anything but an ideal couple.

"For Carol and Chuck Stuart," said the *Globe* in its page one story, "death came at a time rich with potential." It told in melodramatic terms how the infant Christopher had been baptized, commenting that "the ceremony marked the brutal end not just of the couple's dream of family, but of a relationship that by all accounts was so loving it warmed even those at its edge."

Both Carol and Chuck were described in the most glowing terms, substantiated by quotes from co-workers and friends. Kimberley Jaworski, who, along with her husband, worked at Kakas & Sons with Chuck and was friends to both (Chuck, indeed, had been best man at the Jaworskis' wedding and Carol a bridesmaid), was reported as saying that "everyone loved them." Carol was such a devoted daughter, Jaworski added, that she called her mother every night, even when she was on her honeymoon.

Ted Kakas, co-owner of the fur company where Chuck was general manager, went on record as calling Chuck a "terrific guy," the kind of thoughtful person who collected donations for orphans every Christmas and at Thanksgiving organized a food collection program for the needy.

In case anyone had missed the point about random violence, Jacobs also interviewed relatives and neighbors who had warned Chuck and Carol about venturing into the inner city. Mike Stuart, one of Chuck's younger brothers, was quoted as saying how he had warned Chuck about the dangerous neighborhood. "I told him I didn't like parking my car around there, and I would never send my wife in there by herself."

A neighbor of Chuck and Carol's in Medford told the *Globe:* "I wouldn't go into Boston if you gave me $100,000. It's just not safe."

Although there would be many thousands of words written and broadcast about Carol and Chuck in coming weeks and months, future news coverage would basically conform to the pattern set in those first few stories. Remarkably, too, despite efforts by scores of reporters, few hard facts would be unearthed about Chuck or Carol or the crime. When there was a change, it was a very dramatic one, but that would not occur for a long time. Meanwhile the story—and the personalities of the two main participants—became an almost daily event for Bostonians.

Chapter 4

Within hours of the incident, the shooting of Carol and Chuck Stuart had captured the attention, and the sympathy, of millions of people around the world. The story about what happened to them was on the level of the sad tale about the female jogger who was attacked in New York's Central Park: it was horrifying, and it had happened to two such nice, innocent people.

As interest in Chuck and Carol grew, the public clamored for more details about the victims themselves. The media were happy to oblige. The *Herald* dubbed them "the Camelot couple," and the *Globe* indulged in its own form of hyperbole. Over time, reporters began to flesh out the images of the two young people whose faces smiled out from front pages and TV screens on a daily basis.

Carol Ann was the younger of Giusto and Evelyn DiMaiti's two children. Born in the suburb of Medford, which is just north of Boston, she grew up in a typical Italian-American household. Good Catholics, Giusto and Evelyn insisted that Carol attend parochial school, which she did until the one in her neighborhood closed and she had to transfer to public schools. She was in the sixth grade then.

Always a good student and a popular, cheerful girl, Carol made lots of friends, both among her fellow students and her teachers. In her senior year she was elected class treasurer, a tribute both to her personality and her industriousness.

Her father, Giusto, had been a workingman all his life and was a strong believer in the work ethic for his children as well. By the time Carol was in her mid-teens she got a job in a restaurant in Revere, a heavily Irish blue-collar town east of Medford. She started as a busgirl, progressed to a waitress, and then was promoted to hostess. In her spare time, she dated a classmate and fellow Italian-American from Medford, Jeff Cataldo.

Like Carol, Jeff was hardworking and eager to better himself. He too realized that the ticket to long-lasting success in the modern world was a college degree, and he was determined to get his. Giusto liked this in the young man, and he beamed whenever Carol brought him around. In Giusto's eyes Jeff was smart, ambitious, and, not a small thing to consider, a good Italian boy. Carol dated Jeff throughout her final years of high school, and she continued dating him long after she had enrolled at Boston College, a Catholic institution, with the announced intention of becoming a high school teacher like her brother, Carl.

When she got down to the realities of a teacher's life, however, Carol began to have second thoughts.

As an extrovert supreme, she was much more interested in the "real" world than in the somewhat cloistered existence of teaching. Halfway through BC, she switched her major to political science and began considering the law. She was an honor student, one of the prizes in her class, a woman on the way up.

But although she was doing well in school, her personal life began to suffer. Perhaps fearing what marriage to a young Italian man in conservative Medford might mean to a young Italian woman— maybe an early end to a promising career—her romance with Jeff Cataldo began to cool. Giusto was disappointed, but he still had hope. If he could have waved a wand and found a husband for Carol, that man would have been Jeff Cataldo.

Exhausted by the college grind and feeling the need to earn some money before she could go on to law school, Carol decided to take a year off after she graduated. Her father was working as a night bartender at a restaurant in Revere called the Driftwood, and he found her a job there as a waitress. She accepted it gladly.

Working at the Driftwood as a cook was a young man just slightly younger than she, a tall, dark-haired youth with a winning smile and a shy manner. His name was Charles Stuart, Jr., but everyone called him Chuck. When he was a kid growing up in Revere, he was "Charlie," but now that he was on the way up he thought "Chuck" sounded more sophisticated.

Chuck Stuart's childhood had not been that different from Carol's. His father, Charles Sr., was a slap-'em-on-the-back, tell-'em-a-joke boisterous

Irishman; like Carol, he was a highly developed extrovert who seemed to need contact with other people to survive. When he wasn't working as a salesman for Metropolitan Life, he tended bar and emceed gatherings at the local Knights of Columbus hall. And when he wasn't busy doing those things, he helped raise money for the Children's Hospital or the local Little League. It was a good thing he enjoyed extracurricular activities because, in his case, an outside job probably was a necessity as well as an avocation. He had to moonlight somewhere: he had a large family to feed.

When Charles Sr. was a young man, he married a woman named Neysa Robinson. She bore him a child, a girl they named Shelly, in 1953. In 1955 she became pregnant again, but serious health complications set in. She died in childbirth a few months later, but the baby, another girl, survived. Charles Sr. named the infant Neysa, after her mother.

For a while Charles Sr. tried raising the two girls on his own and being a breadwinner at the same time. But it was a difficult life, and he decided to take another wife. The new Mrs. Stuart was Dorothy Kingston, a first-generation American of pure Irish stock. In 1959 they started their own family. A week before Christmas they had a son: Charles Jr. In fairly quick order three other sons followed. Michael came along two years after Chuck. A year after Michael there was Mark, and three years after that, the baby of the family, Matthew. Partly because of the four-year age gap between the oldest son, Chuck, and the youngest daughter, Neysa, the Stuart children grew up almost as separate families: the girls went one way, the boys another. Male bonding took an early hold among the Stuart boys, and while they were growing up, they were almost inseparable. As the oldest, Chuck had a certain responsibility to look after his brothers, which he apparently did, but he also was the shyest of the four and seemed the slowest to make new friends.

As a boy Chuck did most of the things that other Irish kids did in a town like Revere: he took a great interest in sports, and he paid tribute to the church. Like Carol, he went to parochial school. And, like Carol, he was elected class treasurer. But Immaculate Conception was only a grammar school, and when he entered the ninth grade he too transferred to a public school. Unlike Carol, however, Chuck was not a scholar, and his ambitions did not extend to educational achievement. When he was in the tenth grade, he transferred out of the academic program and enrolled at Northeastern Metropolitan Regional Vocational High School in Wakefield, popularly known as the "Voke." He was more interested in cooking than calculus, and he signed up in the food service program.

Even though he was going to the Voke instead of a regular high school, he kept active in sports, playing organized baseball (a teammate later described him as a "weak-hitting third baseman") and basketball. From what his friends remember, he was better at basketball than baseball, but he was hampered by weak knees, which kept him from being a skilled rebounder. He also played sandlot football and practically every other sport that came along.

When he graduated from the Voke in 1977, his

first full-time job was as a cook at a hotel in the
north Boston town of Danvers. The hotel was the
Radisson-Ferncroft, which later became the Sheraton-Tara. Throughout this story, fate and coincidence played a strong part. It is, perhaps, coinci-
dental that a Sheraton-Tara played an instrumental
role at the beginning of Chuck's life as an adult,
and a sister hotel, the Sheraton-Tara in Braintree,
which is south of Boston, played an even more
important role at the end of his life.

One of the reasons Chuck took the job at the hotel
was that two of his friends, brothers Bruce and
Brian Parsons, were working there as well. Brian
was Chuck's best friend then and would remain so
through the years.

While Chuck was working at the hotel, he seriously injured his leg during a pickup football game.
As a result, it was extremely painful for him to have
to stand all day. So he turned in notice at the hotel
and took a few months off to give his injury time to
heal. His next job was as a cook at the Driftwood.

When Carol and Chuck met at the Revere restaurant, which has since closed, they hit it off immediately, and it was not long before they began
dating. Although Carol had been going out with
Jeff Cataldo for several years, Chuck was a novice
at romantic relationships. Until then he had devoted most of his energy to sports, and Carol was
his first serious girlfriend. Although she was almost
halfway through law school and he was only a cook,
they continued to see each other regularly.

The fact that his daughter was dating an Irishman from Revere instead of an Italian boy from Medford did not make Carol's father, Giusto, particularly happy. But like other fathers in similar situations, he came around eventually.

Chuck and Carol met in 1979. On Christmas Eve 1983 Chuck gave Carol a special present: a wallet adorned with her initials—except the initials carved into the leather were C.A.S., not C.A.D. Excitedly she opened the billfold, and inside was a diamond engagement ring, the same one that would, slightly more than six years later, be reported stolen by Chuck.

Carol and Chuck were married on October 13, 1985, at a mass in St. James Catholic Church in Medford, a short walk from the house in which Carol had grown up. The ceremony was performed by the Reverend Francis Gallagher. Chuck once was one of Gallagher's altar boys. The best man was Chuck's old friend, Brian Parsons. Chuck and Carol honeymooned in the Bahamas, and every night Carol called her mother to let her know that everything was all right.

Chuck, who never had either the discipline or the desire to go to college and use that as a ticket to a better job, made an abortive move in that direction in 1979. It was shortly after he met Carol, and perhaps to try to keep up with her, he enrolled at a small school not far from home. But his resolve lasted only two months. Before Thanksgiving he dropped out and never reenrolled. However, there were indications that he felt inferior or guilty about not trying to further his education. Sometimes he told a story about being awarded a football scholarship to Brown University but having to surrender it after suffering a leg injury. When reporters started digging into his life after the shooting, one of them called a Brown official, who denied in the first place that Chuck was ever enrolled there and, in the second place, added that Brown did not give football scholarships.

Despite his lack of interest in higher education, Chuck was nevertheless undeniably ambitious. By 1981, a couple of years after he and Carol started dating, Carol left the restaurant business behind for good and went to work as an accountant for Arthur Young & Co. in Boston. That probably fueled Chuck's need to break out of the cook mold as well, because soon afterward he applied for a job at Kakas & Sons, which had been in business since 1868 and was *the* place to buy furs in Boston. Kakas & Sons may not sell as many mink coats as some of the sophisticated department stores, but the store has a reputation that draws the city's old money.

Under the "education" blank on his job application, Chuck inked in, "Brown University," spinning his yarn about the nonexistent football scholarship. In the end, even if his employers-to-be had checked his claims, it might not have made any difference. The two brothers who were running the store, Ted and Jay, liked the way Chuck presented himself and were impressed with his understated charm. He was hired on the spot as a management trainee.

Soon after that his life-style began to change. Increasingly aware of the need to present a top-notch image at the furrier, where customers paid more attention to service than price tags, Chuck began taking better care of himself. He gave up his barber in Revere for fashionable hairstyling salons. Blue jeans went to the Goodwill, and he started shopping for suits at Brooks Brothers. Casios surrendered to top-of-the-line, $600 imported watches, and his feet soon grew accustomed to finely crafted, hand-rubbed leather shoes.

But some things did not change. Chuck Stuart was effectively out of Revere, but Revere was not altogether out of him. In the world in which he grew up, it was customary for men, once they got old enough to drink, to find themselves a "local" and spend at least one night a week with the "boys," cussin', spittin', fartin', and knockin' back beer after beer. Chuck had never been much of a drinker, but he seemed to relish his Friday nights back in his old hometown. At first Carol didn't mind because she would spend Friday evenings with the girls. Peer bonding, the experts call it. But after Carol got pregnant she cut back on her socializing and seemed to resent Chuck's excursions. It was one of the few constant disagreements they ever had, at least as far as anyone else could see.

By then, though, both had come a long way from the Driftwood.

Chuck had become increasingly more indispensable at Kakas & Sons, and promotion followed promotion. By the late 1980s he had been made the store's general manager, the owners' right-hand man. When Ted or Jay Kakas needed something done, they went first to Chuck, who was ensconced in his own office, albeit a small one, just down the hall from theirs. With the increased reponsibility came increased pay. By 1989 he was taking home six figures, easy.

Life was not entirely trouble free, however. His father had been diagnosed with Parkinson's disease, and deterioration in his physical condition was evident. To make matters worse, doctors had found a lump on his mother's breast, and midway through the year she had a mastectomy. Still the devoted son, Chuck refused to abandon his responsibility. Every month he sent his parents a check for $200. It was the least he could do. There was later speculation that Carol resented these monthly checks and that they often argued about it. That, however, does not fit with Carol's personality. The amount was piddling, considering their combined monthly income, and Carol was such a devoted daughter, she could hardly criticize her husband for helping his parents when they obviously needed assistance. Besides, his siblings were helping as well. Each gave something according to his or her ability. The youngest child, Matthew, for example, although he was twenty-three years old, decided to live at home and help his mother care for his father.

Carol, meanwhile, was also moving up the professional ladder. Although she was settling in well as a tax attorney at the firm she'd left Arthur Young to join, Cahners Publishing Co., she was still looking down the road toward an expanded career. For one thing she decided to go back to school. Someday, she said, she wanted to be a CPA, but for the time being Cahners was treating her well. One of the benefits of her new job was insurance coverage. As an employee she was entitled to an $82,000 policy on her life, which she took.

With Carol what you saw was what you got. Chuck was quiet, almost withdrawn. Even those who knew him well said they often could not tell what he was thinking. It was not uncommon for him to go an hour or so, especially when he was among strangers, and not say a word. Carol was the opposite. She could not keep anything inside; she was compelled to share her thoughts and feelings with everyone. Luckily for those around her, they were almost always happy thoughts. If she saw a pretty flower, she told everyone at work about it. If something someone said made her feel particularly good, she broadcast that as well. On the other hand, if she and Chuck had a spat, she dispensed that information as well. As one co-worker put it, "Carol was the kind of person who would always tell you what she had for breakfast and how it tasted." Some who knew her well would later say they doubted that she and Chuck had any serious disagreements. If they had, they would not have been secrets because Carol would have revealed them.

Soon after Chuck and Carol were married, they bought a small home in Medford. But as their paychecks increased and their life-styles changed, they began thinking in more grandiose terms. When they sold the house they made a tidy $100,000 profit on the deal. Then they had to decide what to do with the money. Although Chuck was drawing a very good salary, he perceived he was about as high as he could go at Kakas & Sons. Although he had left commercial cooking far behind him, he still harbored a desire to open a small restaurant. In his dreams, he confided to those he knew best, he envisioned himself and Brian Parsons running a cozy little eatery where service was even more important than the food and every customer was treated like a friend. He and Carol talked about investing the profit from their house in such a place, but in the end they agreed to postpone such plans. Instead they bought a large split-level home in a more distant suburb, Reading. They agreed to pay $239,000 for the house, and they took out a $177,000 mortgage to clinch the deal.

The new house had plenty of room, which was just what they needed because each had discovered a latent affinity for fancy clothing. Carol took over one room for her dresses and suits, and Chuck appropriated another for his sizable wardrobe. They acquired two frisky Labrador retrievers, Max and Midnight, and they developed an interest in landscaping. Fitness consciousness was a by-product of the yuppie life-style, and they developed their own routines. Carol ran with a neighbor. Chuck joined a health club, where he showed up every morning as religiously as he used to have to appear for early mass at Immaculate Conception when he was an altar boy. In addition to the weight training, Chuck also played in an old-boy basketball league back in Revere. That was the winter sport; in the summer, it was softball. Then, too, there was the time he spent coaching Little Leaguers and refereeing basketball games at Immaculate Conception. Once a week they would go for dinner at the DiMaitis', or the DiMaitis and Stuarts would come to Reading. If the weather was nice, they would sit around the pool. Chuck and Carol also hosted pool parties for their friends. At such functions Chuck likely as not would do the cooking.

During the week, because of the long hours each of them worked, they ate out a lot. Invariably they picked the best restaurants. They vacationed in Europe after Carol expressed a desire to see her ancestral home. And they took less ambitious trips when the mood struck them. Sometimes they went together; sometimes Chuck went with "the boys." Usually these were excursions to sporting events, like the Olympics in Calgary.

Not surprisingly, things changed considerably after Carol got pregnant. When she was in high school, Carol was attributed in her yearbook with having two primary ambitions: becoming a teacher and raising a family. The teacher idea had gone by the wayside, but the desire to have a family was still strong. And at thirty she heard her biological clock ticking loudly. When she discovered she was pregnant, friends said, she was so thrilled that she kept the doctor's report certifying her fecundity for weeks, displaying it proudly to everyone as if it were an award from the pope.

Never one to do things halfway, Carol approached her pregnancy as she had the study of law: wholeheartedly. She modified her exercise program to make sure that her workouts were good for the baby as well as for herself. She gave up alcohol, coffee, and soft drinks with caffeine, developing an almost insatiable desire for caffeine-free colas. She enthusiastically enrolled in the birthing classes at Brigham and Women's and attended the sessions religiously.

Chuck also seemed delighted with the prospect of becoming a father, particularly since Carol's due date coincided so neatly with his own birthday. If she delivered on schedule, it could be both a birthday gift *and* a Christmas present. To show how happy he was with developments, he agreed to surrender the room he had been using to store his considerable wardrobe for a nursery. And he attended the Lamaze classes with Carol. After the shooting, some other students who had been in the class told reporters that while Chuck had been present, he did not speak at all with others in the class, choosing to remain silent while Carol bubbled about the experience. This was not out of character for Chuck; he was not given to overt displays of pseudofriendship with people he did not know.

During the early weeks of Carol's pregnancy, however, Chuck seemed to sense a distancing in his wife's relationship with him. Her focus was changing from him to the baby, and he probably resented it—a not uncommon reaction. And he responded in a not uncommon fashion: he spent even more time with "the guys." His Friday nights out spilled over into Saturday mornings, a situation that Carol apparently objected to vociferously. It is, however, impossible to have a marriage totally without friction, and on the scale of things, this did not appear to be a major problem. If it had been, Carol would most likely have made her unhappiness more evident. Instead, despite the pregnancy, their feelings toward each other did not appear to have changed. Ten days before the shooting occurred, Chuck and Carol spent a long weekend at a luxurious retreat in Connecticut to celebrate their fourth wedding anniversary. From all appearances they *were* the perfect couple. If they had an argument and Carol went to work sour-faced and pouty, her disposition quickly improved when the inevitable flowers arrived from a repentant Chuck.

They were so much in love, friends told the stream of reporters who came looking for chinks in the marriage; they truly cared about each other.

Despite what happened later, and all the things that were splashed in the media, it was hard to believe that there was not more fact that fiction in the closeness of their relationship. It is extremely difficult to believe that someone would not have picked up on the possibility that Chuck and Carol's marriage was not quite as it seemed, that maybe what appeared to be the perfect match was nothing but a carefully constructed facade. Given Carol's proclivity to talk about *everything*, it hardly seems possible that under the surface the relationship between them was seething, literally boiling with hatred. But with only three exceptions, everyone who knew them and has come forward to express their views has said that the marriage was solid. Significantly, perhaps, each of the three who had a tale to tell has been unable to substantiate their claims with witnesses. At least not yet.

Chapter 5

October 26, 1989
Thursday

Physically, Michael Stuart could almost have been Chuck's twin, except Michael was much thinner. At least he was until Chuck went into the hospital and lost fifty pounds. After that the resemblance was startling. They were both tall, slim, reticent, seemingly taciturn men with deeply receding hairlines, thin noses, and hollow cheeks. But what was notable right off was how well Michael, a twenty-seven-year-old firefighter, wore his grief. Maybe it was because of his profession, the fact that he was accustomed to seeing tragedy firsthand; and although it was never a pleasant sight, he realized that catastrophe and contentment were two sides of the same coin. When the family learned about the shooting, Michael was the rock upon which they leaned. Although there were two other older siblings, they were both women. As the oldest male in the family—outside of Chuck, who was fighting for his life, and his father, who was fighting his own desperate battle against a different kind of enemy—it was his responsibility to be stalwart. He owed it to his siblings; he owed it to his parents; he owed it to Chuck.

Given the atmosphere that prevailed, it was not surprising that the youngest child, twenty-three-year-old Matthew, the black sheep of the family, pulled Michael aside, saying he needed to talk. Even though Chuck was the oldest brother, it was always Michael whom Matthew turned to. He was the one Matthew appeared to admire the most, the one he looked up to, the one he wanted to emulate. When Matthew graduated from high school, he had, like his brothers before him, decided that he was not interested in pursuing his education further. Instead, he said, he wanted to be a firefighter like Michael. He took the written exam and scored well, but that was only the first step. There is not much turnover in the Revere Fire Department, and the exam administrator told Matthew that, while his grade was impressive, it might be years before his number came up.

Disappointed, Matthew took a job as a stockboy with a liquor wholesaler, a position that Michael and his other older brother, Mark, had also filled at the beginning of their journey into adulthood.

Although it was a job, the pay was relatively low, and there was no challenge. So Matthew quit to work for a company that cleaned and maintained overhead lighting fixtures. And about midway through 1989 he left that job to become a paint mixer. In that slot he made about $21,000 a year. But that didn't go far in Massachusetts's inflated economy, even considering that he was still living at home. Matthew had other expenses. He liked to spend his evenings in heavy-metal clubs and neighborhood bars, particularly a tavern called Reardon's, which was owned by a cousin. Matthew's half sister, Shelly, worked part-time at Reardon's, and it was a popular family hangout. Chuck liked to go there too whenever he was in Revere. But whereas Chuck drank only enough to be sociable, Matthew had a reputation as a heavy drinker and as somewhat of a hell-raiser when he was blitzed. According to an acquaintance quoted by the *Globe*, Matthew also did a little coke now and then. The newspaper also quoted an unnamed Revere policeman as saying that Matthew was regarded in his hometown as a known drug user.

That may have been one of the reasons that Chuck and Matthew had not gotten along very well in recent years—that and their obviously dissimilar life-styles. Chuck lived in a buttoned-down world, one of expensive suits and expensive haircuts. Matthew was not attracted by either; he seldom wore a suit, and he seldom cut his hair. Hair, in fact, was an issue between them. When Chuck and Carol were married in 1985, Chuck was so enraged by Matthew's long locks that he threatened to kick him out of the wedding party unless he visited a barber.

That was only one of the disagreements they had. Chuck didn't like Matthew's life-style and warned him to shape up. Matthew told him to take a hike. In 1987 they stopped speaking to each other after

Matthew failed to show up to do some work for Chuck as he had promised. As far as the meticulous and demanding Chuck was concerned, that was the ultimate irresponsible act.

Michael had thought the two brothers still were not getting along, which made him even more surprised when Matthew told him that he and Chuck had an arrangement. Exactly what Matthew told Michael that Thursday after the shooting is not clear since the two brothers have been almost completely silent on the issue. Speaking through his attorney, Michael has said only that Matthew came to him and confided that Chuck was personally, directly involved in Carol's murder, and Matthew was involved too in a less direct way.

What went through Michael's mind when he heard that is not known. What is known is that he made a decision to keep the information from the authorities. It is a mystery as to how much information he actually had. Another conundrum is whether or not he confronted Chuck with this information. As close as the Stuart siblings were, it is difficult to believe he did not force a confrontation. But once developments began taking a turn for the worse, the Stuarts withdrew into a shell and refused to discuss with anyone how much they knew or did not know and when they knew it. If that information is ever going to be revealed, it probably will have to be through an investigative authority with subpoena power and the capacity to demand testimony under oath. If Matthew and Michael made a pact of silence, it was not a terribly binding one. It held for a few weeks, and when it was broken, it was broken, ironically, by Matthew, who had the most to lose. If such a bargain existed, and it likely did, Michael kept his part until the whole world knew about it.

At the time Matthew was confiding in Michael, Chuck was confiding in no one. Still under heavy medication and close medical supervision in the intensive care unit at BCH, Chuck asked for a paper and pencil so he could write a message to be read at his wife's funeral. In a hand so shaky Brian Parsons would barely be able to read it, Chuck scribbled a melodramatic good-bye to the woman he had known for ten years and been married to for four.

And as Chuck was penning his eulogy and Matthew was confessing to Michael, a small army of police was spreading out through Mission Hill searching for the man so minutely described by Chuck only hours earlier. At that point Chuck's story still looked good. It had a few holes in it, but the one factor that gave it a truthful ring was the seriousness of Chuck's wounds. If someone was going to shoot himself, the police reasoned, he certainly wouldn't do it as Chuck had done. For weeks that one fact would continue to balance the scale in Chuck's favor despite a growing uneasiness with the details of his story. There was one other thing that helped Chuck's believability quotient: twenty-four hours earlier, determined searchers, eyes fixed on the ground, all but oblivious to the bright autumn sky, found the keys to Carol's Toyota. They were lying in plain view in an empty lot precisely where Chuck had told them the shooting had taken place. After the keys were found, police summoned public service workers to search the sewers and storm drains for the weapon. It did not turn up, and it would not for many weeks. When the gun finally was found, it would be miles away from Mission Hill.

If they couldn't find the gun right away, police at least hoped to find a suspect. From all appearances, police had bought Chuck's story whole. And from what he had said, officers surmised that the man who had shot the two was not an amateur, that he had committed that type of crime before or one very similar to it, such as armed robbery. To them, the cold-bloodedness it took to shoot two unarmed and nonthreatening people, one of them a pregnant woman, reflected a considerable amount of desperation and lack of respect for human life.

As was becoming customary, Boston officials continued to treat the investigation as a political issue as much as a criminological one. Police Superintendent Saia, after announcing at a news conference that the list of suspects had been whittled down to "a chosen few," used the opportunity afforded by the gathering of reporters to make a plea for stronger federal gun control legislation and urge swift passage of a bill in the state legislature to restrict the sale and use of assault weapons.

Also getting into the act were Governor Dukakis and Attorney General James Shannon, both of whom asked for additional funding for crime prevention programs. It might even take new taxes to bring in the needed revenue, Dukakis said, but it was necessary nevertheless. "Drugs and violence are part of our lives, and whether or not we're going to control them or they're going to control us depends on whether we have the will and the courage to commit resources to police and law enforcement."

Attorney General Shannon made his point in an open letter to George Keverian, speaker of the state house of representatives. "We are being overwhelmed by the other side, by the guns, by the violence, and by the crime," he wrote. "We don't have the resources to deal with these problems."

While Dukakis and Shannon were still able to beat the law enforcement drum, Mayor Flynn, who had been first on the find-Carol's-killer train, was starting to take some serious flak because of his aggressive stance. Louis Elisa, president of the city's NAACP chapter and a frequent Flynn critic, attacked the mayor for supporting a double standard in pursuing a vigorous chase for the assailant. "It clearly makes a difference that it's a white suburban couple," Elisa railed. "You're looking at 101 people injured with weapons in Roxbury, and he didn't feel it was necessary to call in all the detectives for that."

It was only the beginning. In the following weeks Flynn would take a much heavier battering.

But Flynn was not the only target of criticism. Media bashers were beginning to raise their voices as well. Even then, as early as three days after the shooting, even before the media saturation *really* began, a number of Bostonians were already starting to question the extensive coverage being given the case. Was it just because the victims were affluent? they asked. Was it just because the crime happened in the inner city? Was it (shades of Elisa's accusations) just because they were *white*?

The *Globe,* as a good newspaper was required to do, addressed some of these questions. But the story by staff reporter Eileen McNamara was relegated to the Metro section in the back of the newspaper. The front page was reserved for developments in the investigation.

WHEN TRAGEDY IS MEASURED BY RACE, CLASS, read the headline on McNamara's piece. The text carried the thought further: "Elements of race and class had many in Greater Boston debating yesterday why some tragedies loom larger than others, why some lives violently lost bring demands for the death penalty and others yield only private, familial grief."

McNamara pointed out how, in contrast with the publicity over the attack against Chuck and Carol, the murder of a black man in a nearby neighborhood a few hours later rated zero on the attention scale. "There were no cameras clicking, no minicams rolling at the city morgue when Sandra Williams identified the body of the man who shared her apartment," McNamara wrote. "No news conferences were convened to mark a lone black man's passing." The reporter then quoted a bitter Sandra Williams: "No mayor called about my loss."

The story also quoted the photo editor at the competing *Herald,* Kevin Cole, who said he had been besieged with complaints about the newspaper's decision to print a picture of Chuck and Carol slumped on the front seat of their Toyota, a picture that later would be shown around the world. But Cole said he'd got no calls when a few days previously the newspaper had printed a picture of a fifteen-year-old black boy who had been shot dead while riding his bicycle.

Ben Haith, identified as a community activist, said the media responded, as it should have, when an eleven-year-old black girl named Darlene Tiffany Moore was shot to death in a crossfire in Roxbury a year earlier. "But for most crimes," he added, "if the victim is white, there seems to be a big difference." For example, he asked rhetorically, where were the media more recently when members of a black gang shot up a black revival center during a service?

McNamara pointed out that the Stuart case was not the first instance where the media's motives were questioned. In 1976, the story asked, did the media underplay an incident in which a white man was beaten by blacks because it came at a time of high racial tension? By the same token, did news reports overplay an assault on a black lawyer who was stabbed with an American flag on City Hall Plaza? And how about cases involving the slaying of a Harvard football star who was killed in a district known as the Combat Zone in 1977? And the rape/murder of a white nurse by two black men in 1981?

In the end, McNamara concluded, no one had any answers. But even if the Stuart shootings were hyped, said Haith, it may prove worth it in the long run if it spurred officials into action to help stop the spread of drugs.

In addition to the moral, the secular, the official, and the philosophical planes on which the story was by then moving, there was one more to be heard from: the religious.

The night before, a Catholic service had been held for Carol at Mission Church, a few blocks from where Chuck had pulled off to the side to wait for police and paramedics to find him. The Reverend Joseph F. Krastel, who had never met Carol or Chuck, asked the three hundred-plus Mission Hill residents who had jammed the church to pray not only for Carol and the members of her family, but for themselves as well. "This evening, as we try to console the Stuart family, we must also ask God to help us, for we are desperate," he said, referring to the prevailing atmosphere that made such a crime possible.

His concerns were echoed by State Representative Kevin Fitzgerald, who represents Mission Hill. "We are here not only to share our concern, sadness, and prayer for the Stuart family, but to all victims of senseless violence."

Mission Hill, as a result of the shooting of Chuck and Carol rather than past deficiencies, was being asked to accept a heavy load of guilt, to bare itself to the world as a lawless jungle. It would prove itself up to the responsibility. But other players in other scenarios would not. Not even seventy-two hours had passed since McLaughlin had answered Chuck's call, but already the situation was fragmenting into clearly defined problem areas. As time passed, those areas would become even more sharply defined, and the situation would become even more fragmented. There were three shots fired in Carol Stuart's Toyota that October night. Only three, but the damage they did was beyond comprehension. Not only had they taken one life (it soon would become two, then three), but like the bullet that ripped through Chuck's abdomen, damaging everything in its path, the results of events precipitated by the shooting would rip through Boston's social, moral, political, legal, and racial stratas, creating wounds that might never be repaired.

October 28, 1989
Saturday

The memorial service at Mission Church, as touching as it was, was only the preliminary. The main event was Carol's funeral. More than eight hundred people turned out on the bright Saturday morning for the service at St. James Church in Medford. It was the same church in which she and Chuck had been married 1,475 days earlier. And it was the church in which Chuck and Carol's baby would have been baptized if October 23 had not happened.

It seemed as though everyone who was anyone was there. Packed into the church along with family members and close friends were Governor Dukakis, Mayor Flynn, Police Commissioner Roache, Cardinal Bernard Law, who was dressed in full regalia complete with cope and miter, and scores of city and state officials. Off to one side, inconspicuous among the brighter lights, was a striking, athletic-looking blonde named Debbie Allen, a twenty-two-year-old graduate student who had worked with Chuck at Kakas & Sons for a couple of summers. On that day she melted into the background. In a short time she would have her picture splashed across the newspapers and flashed on TV screens.

Chuck, of course, was not there. He was still in the intensive care unit at BCH. But when the time came, Brian Parsons, looking weary and old beyond his years, read the farewell message his friend had written. "Good night, sweet wife, my love," he read, squinting to decipher Chuck's wavy penmanship. "God has called you to his hands, not to take you away from me . . . but to bring you away from the cruelty and violence that fill this world." Among the mourners, the tears flowed copiously. Deeply moved himself, Parsons continued in a wavering voice, reading how Chuck was moved by Carol's ability to bring joy and kindness to everyone. When he finished, the church was silent, except for sobs that rose and fell like waves on the beach.

When the brief service was over, the pallbearers marched forward. Among them, distinguished by his shoulder-length curly hair and erect bearing, was Matthew Stuart. Within hours he would depart for California. Why he left Boston is uncertain. He *said* it was a long visit to his girlfriend's relatives. In any case, he did not return to Massachusetts until mid-December, some six weeks later. And by that time all hell was breaking loose.

Chapter 6

While their bosses took time out to go to the funeral, the workaday cops continued their massive and relentless search for a violent, raspy-voiced suspect. The first to be publicly mentioned as a likely candidate was a recent prison escapee, but his name disappeared as quickly and mysteriously as it appeared. The next to surface was a hapless druggie and former hard-timer named Alan Swanson.

The twenty-nine-year-old Swanson, a poorly educated black who grew up in housing projects in New York and Boston, had three things going against him: 1) He was in the Mission Hill project when Chuck and Carol were shot; 2) he was living in an apartment that was not his; and 3) he owned a black sweatsuit.

Swanson was no stranger to police. In the not-too-distant past he served time in Walpole State Prison for armed robbery. While there, one of the friends he made among the inmates was another black man from Boston who was doing time for pulling a gun on a police officer. That prisoner's name was William Bennett; his friends called him "Willie." It was a friendship that would last over the years. Before long Swanson and Bennett would be closer together than they ever wanted to be.

Early in October, Swanson didn't have a place to stay, so a friend said he could use his apartment in Mission Hill. Gratefully Swanson, his girlfriend, and their three children moved in.

On the day after Chuck and Carol were shot, several of Swanson's old prison buddies came by to tell him to keep a low profile because he fit the general description of the alleged Stuart attacker and police were looking to arrest somebody. One of those who made a special trip to warn him, Swanson said later, was Willie Bennett.

"That's cool," Swanson told them all. "I'm going to get in that apartment, and I ain't going nowhere."

He didn't have to. The police came to him. Without warning, he said, a squad of police burst through the door and told him he was under arrest on a charge of breaking and entering, apparently because he was found in an apartment in which he was not supposed to be.

Even at that stage, Swanson said, he was not too worried. But an iceball formed in his stomach when one grim-faced officer came out of the bathroom and gave him a hateful glance. "He's the one," the officer muttered. Soaking in a plastic bucket in the bathroom was a black jogging suit.

The suit fit the description of the clothing Chuck had said his attacker wore all right, except for one minor difference. Chuck had said the assailant's suit had a red stripe. Swanson's suit had a white stripe. Apparently that didn't matter.

According to the *Globe*, the detective who ordered Swanson's arrest, Paul J. Murphy, had to make a formal request for a search warrant before he could confiscate the garment. When Murphy drew up his request for a judge to sign, he stated that he wanted to search for a black jogging suit with "red *or white* stripes" (italics added).

Swanson was dragged off to jail, and as he explained in an interview to *Globe* staffer Sean Murphy, that is where his troubles really began.

Although he was being held for breaking and entering, not for murdering Carol and shooting Charles, the jail grapevine quickly had him pegged as the gunman. From then on, he said, it was a constant round of harassment from both guards and fellow prisoners. They taunted him ceaselessly, he said, and made sure he didn't eat because by the time his food tray got to him he discovered that someone had always spit in it. He was saved from starvation, he figured, by a few good friends who slipped him junk food from the jail canteen.

Ten days after he was arrested, his court-appointed lawyer demanded a trial. By that time the original B&E charge had been upgraded to unarmed burglary. But just before he went into court, it was inexplicably reduced to simple trespassing. He was found not guilty, but before he could be released he was charged with another crime: armed robbery.

After another ten days he was tried on that charge. The man whom Swanson had allegedly held up refused to testify during the proceeding, claiming that police had intimidated him to make him sign the complaint against Swanson.

In the meantime, another man had been arrested, and he was considered a more likely suspect than Swanson in the Stuart shootings. Because they had someone else to focus on, police lost interest in Swanson and he was no longer considered a suspect. The armed robbery charge was dropped, and he was released.

You could have knocked him over with a match, Swanson said, when he heard the name of the new suspect. It was his old friend from Walpole and, more lately, Mission Hill: Willie Bennett.

If all of life's losers were to be gathered in a single huge room, Willie Bennett would have a reserved seat on the first row.

A thirty-nine-year-old ne'er-do-well with a grudge against policemen, Bennett has been a problem for law enforcement officers since he was fourteen.

A not-too-bright student who was having a rough time in school to begin with, Bennett dropped out in the seventh grade and took to the streets. His first recorded arrest was in January 1964, when the fourteen-year-old was picked up for robbing parking meters. Five months later he was arrested again for stealing a woman's purse. Over the next few years he built a sizable record for minor crimes. But in 1973 he moved into the big leagues when he was sentenced to six years for shooting a policeman in the leg.

According to a Mike Barnicle column, Bennett and another man decided to rob a taxi driver. The man had only forty-two dollars, and that apparently made Bennett angry. So he demanded the man's shoes, too. When the driver was slow to comply, Bennett allegedly shot him in the stomach. Later he discovered that the man couldn't give him his shoes because he didn't have any. He was an amputee.

Two years later, in 1981, Bennett was stopped for a traffic violation and decided not to accept the ticket. When the officer offered the paper to Bennett, Bennett reached under the seat of his car and came up with a shotgun. Relieving the officer of his pistol, he shot out the front tire of the patrol car so he couldn't be followed, threatened to shoot the cop if he tried to do anything, and sped off. Three months later police tracked Bennett to where he was staying in the apartment of a friend. When the officers burst through the door, Bennett scooped up a .357 Magnum and screamed, "You ain't taking me alive!" Before he could fire, one of the officers, in a scene straight out of a John Wayne movie, shot Bennett in the hand. Bennett was eventually sentenced to seven years for assault and armed robbery.

In retrospect it was almost inevitable that he would not be at least questioned in connection with the Stuart incident. In the early days of the investigation, police still were thinking that the attack was perpetrated by someone who had a record of violent crimes. As a matter of routine, they combed their records for people meeting that profile. Not surprisingly, Bennett's name surfaced very quickly. Unfortunately for Bennett, his name was already in the mill.

Three weeks before Chuck and Carol were shot, a black man wearing a red baseball cap, a blue jacket, and jeans had sauntered into a video store on Boylston Avenue in the Brookline neighborhood, which is not far from Mission Hill. Glaring at the clerk, he whipped a snub-nosed, nickel-plated revolver from his pocket. "I want everybody here," he said, waving the terrified clerk into a corner. Summoning the store manager and a luckless customer, he ordered them, along with the clerk, to lie spread-eagle on the floor. "I'm going to kill you all," he growled, reaching into the cash register drawer. While they trembled in anticipation of instant death, the robber scooped up the money—$642, it turned out—spun around, and dashed out the door. When asked later if the robber had any distinguishing physical characteristics, the victims said that, as a matter of fact, he did. He had a scruffy beard and a raspy voice.

Ah-ha, thought the police. Listen to this: Baseball cap. Black man. Scruffy beard. Raspy voice. Snub-nosed, nickel-plated revolver. Armed robber. Little apparent regard for life. Right age bracket. Same general size and weight. He sounded like a strong suspect to them. But there was more.

Bennett had a nephew named Joey Bennett, who lived in Mission Hill. The fifteen-year-old Joey was something of a braggart. And he liked to boast about his uncle's exploits.

Joey Bennett had a friend named Dereck Jackson. On October 24, the day after the Stuart shootings, the seventeen-year-old Jackson, who also lived in Mission Hill, went to visit his friend Joey. While he was there a man he did not know came in, and Joey introduced him as his uncle Willie. What occurred next is a little confusing because there are conflicting stories. But based on what those involved have said so far, it happened like this:

A few minutes after he arrived, Joey told Jackson he had something he wanted to show him. He took him into his bedroom and displayed some newspaper clippings detailing the more spectacular of his uncle Willie's brushes with the law.

Jackson, remembering that morning's news broadcasts, then asked, "Did he do the Stuarts, too?"

"Yeah," Joey Bennett replied, laughing heartily.

The next day, Jackson recalled, he ran into another friend, eighteen-year-old Eric Whitney. Bursting with the information he had learned about Joey's uncle, Jackson breathlessly related the details of his visit to Whitney.

It happened, however, that Whitney's mother, Maralynda, was having a romantic relationship with a police officer named Trent Holland. Whitney told his mother about Joey's uncle Willie. She told Holland. He passed the information on to Detective Peter J. O'Malley, who was investigating the Stuart shootings.

Soon after his unfortunate meeting with Whitney, Jackson was summoned to the homicide division headquarters to meet with O'Malley. When he arrived he found Whitney and his girlfriend also there.

Alone in a room with O'Malley, Jackson said he told the detective what had happened in Joey's apartment, adding that he thought Joey had been joking about his uncle Willie's involvement. According to Jackson, O'Malley called him a liar, saying he had heard a different story from Whitney. Jackson said the detective then threatened to file charges against him that could result in a twenty-year prison term.

"Let me take a lie detector test," a frightened Jackson pleaded. "That'll show I'm telling the truth."

According to Jackson, O'Malley stared at him angrily and said the closest he would get to a lie detector would be to be thrown into a small room with a large policeman.

O'Malley, according to Jackson, then called Whitney into the room. With Whitney present, Jackson said he was asked to repeat his version of what had happened in Joey's apartment. When he denied that he had heard Willie Bennett confess, Whitney interrupted him.

"No, no, Dee," Whitney said, implying that was not the way it happened.

Frightened by the threat of prison and a beating, and with the knowledge that his friend apparently had told a different tale, Jackson said he then told another story about hearing Willie Bennett confess. O'Malley, satisfied, asked Jackson to repeat his second story into a tape recorder. Then, he said, O'Malley gave him a twenty-dollar bill and told

him to go celebrate. That, at least, was Dereck
Jackson's version of the sequence of events; O'Malley has not answered the accusations. However,
District Attorney Newman Flanagan has denied the
charges.

The next step was for O'Malley to get a warrant for
Bennett's arrest and a paper allowing him to
search the apartment where Bennett was believed
to be staying, along with his mother's apartment
in Mission Hill. In applying for the warrant, O'Malley cited the statements by Dereck Jackson and
Eric Whitney that implicated Bennett. But the detective had other ammunition as well. Tucked in
his jacket pocket were two additional statements,
one from a twenty-year-old woman named Tony
Jackson and other from a high school student
named David Brimage.

According to O'Malley, the woman, Tony Jackson,
told him that she had heard Bennett as much as
admit shooting Chuck and Carol. What Bennett
was alleged to have said was: "The bullet was not
meant for the lady; it was meant for the man."

And the high school student was said to have
sworn that he heard Joey Bennett admit that his
uncle had done the shooting.

But Jackson and Brimage were frosting on the
cake. O'Malley was relying on what he said Dereck
Jackson and Eric Whitney told him as the foundation for his request for the warrants against Bennett. In his request, O'Malley said Jackson provided
a plethora of details about what Bennett was alleged to have said. For instance, Bennett was sup-

posed to have admitted before the small group of
youths in Joey Bennett's apartment that he had
ordered Stuart to keep his eyes on the road and not
to look in the rearview mirror. Those were the
magic words: "Do not look in the rearview mirror."
Police had not revealed that Chuck had told them
that. Those words were something they were hold-
ing back to help separate the wheat from the chaff
when they questioned suspects. That is normal
procedure in police departments everywhere: they
want to be able to say that a suspect is genuine
because he could not possibly have learned a certain fact from reading the newspapers. In this case,
the fact that Jackson allegedly used those particular words added considerable weight to O'Malley's
application. Jackson also was supposed to have
heard Bennett claim that he had been wearing a
"black Adidas jumpsuit" at the time, and this also
fit with Chuck's description of the attacker.

"Jackson also stated," O'Malley wrote in what
apparently was designed as the kicker to his request, "that Willie Bennett then demonstrated
with the gun in his hand how he had shot them."

The detective's argument was persuasive. Suffolk
Superior Court Judge John J. Irwin, Jr., signed the
warrants.

By this time the case was becoming even more
emotional; the roller coaster was still going up. On
Thursday, November 9, at 4:34 P.M., baby Christopher Stuart died at Brigham and Women's Hospital. Age, seventeen days. Weight, three pounds thirteen ounces. Although it is not unusual for babies

born two months premature to survive, the fact that Christopher had apparently been without oxygen for some thirty minutes before he was delivered seemed to have proved too much of a barrier to overcome. Chuck, who was still being treated at BCH, had been notified earlier that Christopher's death seemed imminent. Apparently shaken by the news, he asked to be transported by ambulance to Brigham and Women's so he could see his child. In a dramatic meeting in the hospital's intensive care unit, Chuck cried over the infant before he was taken back to his own hospital bed.

Christopher's death was ruled a homicide to fulfill a legal requirement. If his death were to be judged a murder, then whoever killed his mother could be charged with a second slaying. The official report listed the cause of death as complications stemming from his mother's gunshot wound.

This was almost more drama than Bostonians could take. Progress reports on Chuck's and Christopher's conditions and the status of the investigations were a daily staple for news junkies, who sopped up all the details provided and clamored for more. When Christopher died, the pressure on police to make an arrest magnified immensely. Undoubtedly that played some part in O'Malley's plans. If nothing else, it made his efforts more urgent. On the night of November 11, a Saturday, about fifty-two hours after Christopher's death, O'Malley, with warrants in hand, ordered simultaneous raids on the apartments of Bennett's girlfriend and his mother.

The girlfriend, Faye Nelson, lived in Burlington. Bennett's mother, a tiny white-haired woman, lived in Alton Court in Mission Hill. Police officers knew Bennett sometimes stayed there. They also knew that Alton Court was only a short walk from the spot where Chuck said he and his wife were attacked.

Officers found Bennett in his girlfriend's place. Cuffing him quickly, they bundled him into a squad car and rushed him off to be booked, photographed, fingerprinted, and tossed into a cell. As badly as they wanted to charge him with the murders of Carol and Christopher, they had no physical evidence to do so. So they kept him instead on armed robbery charges relating to the robbery of the Brookline video store.

Bennett claimed that he was with his girlfriend on the night Carol and Chuck were shot. That would have been hard to disprove, particularly considering the fact that police had recovered neither a black sweatsuit nor a pistol. But then something happened that made it even worse for the unlucky Bennett. No sooner had he sworn to interrogators that he was with Faye Nelson when Carol and Chuck were shot than his two sisters volunteered to a reporter that he had been with *them* that night. Contradicting their brother, they alleged that the three of them were in the Parker Street Lounge, a sleazy Mission Hill bar, on an errand for their mother when Chuck and Carol were accosted a few blocks away.

To the police, it was a laugh. Sure, said the skeptical cops. Here's a guy with a long rap sheet who fits the description of the Stuart assailant saying he was with his girlfriend in Burlington. But his *sisters* say they were somewhere else. The least they could do was get their stories straight, they must have thought. What they said was, While you work out your alibi we're going to keep Willie Bennett in the slammer.

Chapter 7

Bennett's arrest appeared to be the beginning of a satisfactory conclusion to a drama that had held people around the world enthralled for almost a month. In fact, it was only the beginning of a situation that would get more tangled and confused by the day. And those days would stretch into weeks, then the weeks into months. In hindsight, rather than being the first step toward an illuminating experience in which all would be explained, Bennett's arrest was only a quick peek into a darkened warehouse; for every question it purported to answer, three more unanswered questions popped up. But at the time no one knew that was going to be the case.

Indeed, Bennett's November 11 capture had taken a considerable load off police, who were under tremendous pressure to find a suspect. And he *did* look like a good suspect. He fit precisely the physical description Chuck had given of his attacker, a fact that still has not been not fully explained. But he not only looked like the person Chuck had said shot him and his wife, he matched the psychological profile as well. In addition, as far as the public knew, there were solid witness reports linking Bennett to the attack. Although Bennett was being held only on armed robbery charges and not for the murders of Carol and Christopher, police department leaks unquestionably implied that he was then the prime—in fact, the only remaining—suspect in the case.

Predictably, Bennett's family leaped to his defense, claiming he was being framed because of his long criminal record and his history of violence. But it was hard to argue these claims successfully when Faye Nelson was telling one story about his whereabouts on the night of the Stuart attack and two of his sisters were telling a contradictory one. Plus, there were the statements from Dereck Jackson, Eric Whitney, Tony Jackson (who was not related to Dereck), and David Brimage. Maybe there were others, some that have not surfaced even yet. In any case, police seemed convinced that they had a good case despite the lack of physical evidence. If Bennett had been the assailant, one would expect him, after all, to get rid of the pistol and incriminating jogging suit.

How closely Bennett fit the other two criteria that made his description unique—the patchy beard and raspy voice—is still not known. When Bennett appeared to be arraigned on armed robbery charges relating to the holdup in Brookline, he was clean-shaven. And since he did not speak, it is not on the record if he talks in a raspy, singsong voice. In any case, the victims of the Brookline robbery identified Bennett as the man who held up the video store. Since they presumably saw him before his November 13 arraignment, it may be that he was not clean-shaven when they got a look at him. Whether they heard him talk or not is not known. There was speculation in the *Globe* on November 13 that investigators would seek a court order compelling Bennett to provide a sample of his voice, but whether that ever came about is not known. Such a plan may simply have fallen through the cracks in the wave of developments that were soon to come.

On October 30, a week after the shooting and almost two weeks before Bennett's arrest, investigators visited Chuck at BCH and showed him pictures of twenty men they then regarded as suspects. It is not known whether Bennett's picture was in that stack or what Chuck's reaction was to the photos.

November 13, 1989
Monday

Globe ombudsman Robert L. Kierstead, in a column that appeared on the newspaper's op-ed page, addressed reader complaints that the *Globe* had been derelict in not immediately printing a racial description of the man who allegedly shot Chuck and Carol. An ombudsman's duty at a newspaper is to act as a reader's advocate on questions of editorial decision making. He is, in other words, the reader's pipeline into the newsroom.

"A few of these [complaining] readers felt the description was left out because of the race aspect involved," Kierstead wrote. "Not so. The *Globe* had the race, gender, and approximate height in the [initial] story, but an editor deleted the information because it failed to conform to the newspaper's stylebook guideline." Kierstead then proceeded to explain that the stylebook, the editorial department's bible, specifies that race should be mentioned only when it is pertinent to the story *or* when it is part of a physical description that includes more than just height and gender.

Kierstead went on to say that the newspaper violated its own stylebook on October 25, two days after the shooting, when it published the suspect's height, age, and race. Kierstead even quoted managing editor Thomas Mulvoy as having confessed to the violation. By October 25, Kierstead said, the *Globe* had enough details about other physical characteristics to justify printing the information that the suspect was a black man.

What makes Kierstead's column particularly interesting is that it reflects the racial divisions that soon would become much more pronounced. One group was complaining because the suspect *was not* identified as a black man, another group was complaining because he *was*. Up until then the most vocal complaints had come from Bostonians, notably civil rights leaders and community activists, who protested because newspapers *had* described the alleged attacker as a black man, saying that this was an inflammatory, racist action.

November 15, 1989
Wednesday

A Suffolk County grand jury began its investigation into the attack on Chuck and Carol. Although
grand jury proceedings are secret, word leaked out
that the group was focusing intently on Willie Bennett as the assailant. Both Dereck Jackson and Eric
Whitney were called to testify. Although the public
would not know about it for another six weeks, the
following is what Jackson and Whitney said about
their roles in the proceedings and in what happened immediately before and immediately afterward:

The day after he met with O'Malley and was
pressured into giving a false story, Jackson said, he
called Whitney and suggested the two of them
return to the detective's office and tell them they
had been lying about Bennett's confession.

"Bottom line," Jackson told his friend, "we got
to go back there and tell the truth."

Whitney said he would talk to Trent Holland, his
mother's policeman boyfriend, about setting up a
second meeting. When it came about, he said, he
was kept in one room with Holland and another
officer while Whitney was closeted in a separate
room with O'Malley. One of the officers brought
him a chicken sandwich, and while he was eating
they started telling him about things that could
happen to teenagers in a state penitentiary. Later,
when he and Whitney were put in a room together
alone, Whitney waved under Jackson's nose a form
he claimed was a booking sheet.

"If we don't stick to our stories, we're under

arrest," Whitney said. He glanced around furtively, as though he were afraid of being overheard. "We're not leaving here, Dee," he whispered. "They're talking about twenty years. They're not playing games." Then he looked at Jackson pleadingly. "Dee, I want to leave here. Don't change your story."

Jackson said he left without talking to O'Malley.

But for days afterward he worried about the spot he had gotten himself into. Then, just before he was to appear before the grand jury, he was called into a meeting with an assistant district attorney, who showed him a transcript of the recorded—and untrue—statement he had made to O'Malley.

"Is this true?" the prosecutor asked, brandishing the statement.

"Y-yes," Jackson stammered.

A few minutes later he went into the grand jury room and related what he knew was "a blatant lie."

Frightened about what he had done, Jackson asked for a lawyer. The attorney set up a meeting involving O'Malley, the assistant district attorney who had shown Jackson the statement, the county's chief trial lawyer, and Whitney. At that meeting Whitney admitted he had never heard Bennett confess to shooting the Stuarts.

The next day, Jackson said, he returned to the grand jury and told the group that he had lied in his earlier statement. He made the admission, he said, even though he had been warned by his lawyer that he could be charged with perjury. But he figured it would be worth it if Bennett did not have to go to jail because of his false testimony.

Two days after Dereck Jackson went public with his assertions against the police, Eric Whitney was interviewed by the *Globe*. Whitney told basically the same story as Jackson—that is, that Holland and then O'Malley had threatened him if he did not say what they wanted to hear. The pressure began with Holland, who brought him pictures of Carol Stuart's jewelry. While showing him the photos, Holland also fed Whitney details about what Chuck had said the attacker looked like.

Two days later Whitney was summoned by O'Malley, who told him that if he cooperated, he would help him with two charges pending against him, one for shoplifting and one for destruction of property. If he did not cooperate, O'Malley promised that he would see to it that Whitney got a twenty-year prison term.

When he proved reluctant to swear falsely that he had heard Willie Bennett confess, Whitney said O'Malley lost his temper and waved a paper in his face that appeared to be a form calling for his arrest. At that point he decided to cooperate.

Soon afterward he also appeared before the grand jury, and as Jackson had done, he lied. But, also as Jackson had done, he went back before the group the next day and recanted.

At this stage only Jackson's and Whitney's versions of these events are public. Police have declined to comment on the allegations. Later, District Attorney Flanagan said that the accusations were baseless and self-serving. The grand jury that met on that day has since been disbanded. The group did not make public anything that transpired in its meetings. But neither did it indict Willie Bennett for the murders of Carol and Christopher Stuart. However, a few days later a judge ordered Bennett held under $50,000 bail for the robbery of the Brookline video store. He wasn't going anywhere.

November 20, 1989
Monday

A private funeral service was held for Christopher Stuart. Doctors at BCH decided that Chuck, who had undergone a second operation to help correct the damage caused by the gunshot, was too ill to attend the service.

November 21, 1989
Tuesday

News reports indicate that Chuck was shown a second group of photographs of possible suspects and that he registered a "strong physical reaction" to a picture of Bennett. The reports said that he did not make a positive identification, however.

This is significant because if it happened when the news reports said it did, it was the same day that Dereck Jackson appeared before the grand jury and told his fake story about Bennett. Not until the next day would he (allegedly) go back before the group to tell them he had been lying.

During this whole period, skepticism was building in newsrooms around the city that there was something fishy about Chuck's version of what had happened the night of October 23. When events took a dramatic turn several weeks later, a veritable corps of reporters would come forward saying they had been suspicious of Chuck's story from the beginning but had not been able to convince police to follow through on leads they were uncovering.

For their part, the police said they were following standard investigative procedures, and there was nothing in the early days to indicate that Chuck's story was anything but truthful. Indeed, the single most substantiating factor was the severity of Chuck's wound. In a similar well-known case, that of Army Captain Jeffrey McDonald, a Green Beret convicted of killing his wife and children, some investigators had been suspicious of McDonald's claim that he and his family had been attacked by a pack of hippies because, while the wife and children suffered multiple vicious wounds, McDonald had only scratches. This certainly was not true in Chuck's case.

Also, police said, they were hearing many of the same rumors as those passed on to them by reporters, but they had been no more successful in tracking them down than the journalists. In one case in particular a detective said he had heard a report that Chuck had approached one of his high school buddies several months before the October 23 shooting and asked him if he would kill his wife for him. When the detective called the man and confronted him with the report, the man denied the conversation ever took place.

Reporters said they were having the same difficulties. Not only were they not able to substantiate any of the rumors they had heard, but their job in checking them out was made difficult by the fact that Chuck was a hero. There was so much sympathy for Chuck in the early weeks that any attempt to dig up information that would discredit him was met with hostility.

Another significant factor was the emotional aspect of the story, created in large part by the media: the publication and broadcasting of the conversation between Chuck and Gary McLaughlin, for example, as well as the continuing drama of Chuck's hospitalization, Christopher's fight for life, and the infant's eventual death. And then there was the arrest of the suspect himself. If Bennett had been a more sympathetic figure, the story might have taken a different turn much earlier than it did. But although there was considerable concern for Chuck, it was very difficult to drum up much sympathy for a man who had shot a policeman, cold-bloodedly threatened to shoot another, and then was going to try to shoot his way out of being captured. As a hero, the public was not quite ready to accept a man with at least sixty arrests on his sheet.

But no matter how many journalists said later that they had deep misgivings about Chuck's claims, there was not a single story, column, editorial, or newscast that indicated even the slightest amount of doubt.

Chapter 8

At Boston City Hospital Chuck gained strength rapidly, but it was obvious that the injury had taken its toll. While he once appeared bulky, some might say beefy, he now looked gaunt. The expensive clothes he had selected with care hung on him as though they had been fitted for an older brother. His cheeks were sunken, and his jaw jutted more prominently than ever. But his eyes had regained their old flash, and he could be as imperious as he had been when he was reporting every day as general manager of the city's most prestigious furriers: a colonel who is used to having his commands obeyed.

A steady stream of visitors trooped through his room, mainly his family members and co-workers, and he often sent them off on personal errands. Among the items he asked his brothers to fetch for him were a stack of papers from his safe at home, a pile of files that included insurance policies he had on himself and Carol. What became of those papers would later fuel a spirited debate. Although many people, including investigators, were convinced that Chuck had several policies on Carol's life, they were not able to find the documents themselves, leading to speculation that he secreted at some distant location some of the records his family members innocently delivered to him.

When Chuck was not entertaining visitors in person, he was usually glued to the telephone chatting with friends. One of his frequent callers was a former co-worker he had undoubtedly taken an interest in. Her name was Debbie Allen, and she was a student at Babson College working on an MBA. Allen is the mystery woman in the Stuart saga. A tall, slim woman with a figure skater's taut body and thick blond hair falling below her shoulders, Allen and Chuck may or may not have been romantically involved. They met when Allen, then a student at Brown University, was working summers at Kakas & Sons. Although she would later emphatically deny that she had a romantic relationship with Chuck, there was enough evidence to cause doubt.

Once, when Chuck said he was interested in seeing the chichi prep school she had attended, Allen took him on a tour and introduced him to several of her former teachers. When Allen said she could not afford to call him regularly in the hospital, as Chuck had requested, he gave her his telephone credit card to use. She called virtually daily, and some of their calls lasted for as long as thirty-five minutes. He reportedly bought a $250 gold brooch which he intended to give to Allen, although she claimed the most expensive gift she ever received from him was a pair of sneakers. Apparently they were seen in social situations more than once, but Allen insisted the relationship was platonic.

One argument against the existence of a romantic relationship between Chuck and Allen was that it was doubtful such a liaison could have existed without Carol's knowledge. And if Carol had known about it, she would have talked about it. Yet none of her friends ever indicated that Carol had mentioned any serious problems in her marriage, much less the presence of another woman.

These revelations proved how little the public knew about Chuck Stuart. The headline writers crowned him an all-American youth, a glowing example of kid from a blue-collar background making it on his own, only to have his dream shattered by a nightmarish figure striking in the night. It was a convenient story; a gripping one. It just wasn't true. The true saga of Chuck and Carol is much more complicated than news reports had so far indicated. But by December some of the media-induced gift wrapping was beginning to be peeled away; the story of the Camelot Couple was about to unravel.

Chuck was released from BCH on December 5. For the first time in six weeks he was back on the streets again. Maybe because it was too painful to return to the slate blue split-level home he and Carol had shared, or maybe because he was trying to keep up his image as a devoted son, he went not to Reading, but to Revere, to his parents' little red house nestled at the end of a quiet, dead-end street. By then, however, the media was not pursuing Chuck as heavily; his time in the spotlight had about run its course. There didn't seem to be much else to say. Besides, Chuck had not exhibited any desire to talk to reporters, and journalists had other stories to chase.

Safely out of the media gaze, Chuck picked up his life with virtually uninterrupted anonymity. While no one was looking over his shoulder, one of the first things he did was go into Boston to sign the papers so he could collect on an $82,000 insurance policy that had been taken out on Carol's life through her employer.

As far as the Stuart case went, media interest had shifted from Chuck to Willie Bennett, who was still looking strong as the gunman. The question of the day was, Would Bennett be indicted for the murders of Carol and Christopher? Crucial to an indictment was his identification by Chuck as the assailant. Up to that time Chuck had not seen Bennett in person, and his last publicly known contact with an identification process was the group of photos he had been shown two weeks earlier, on November 21.

Almost a month previously, after the grand jury had begun hearing testimony in the Stuart case, the group had ordered Bennett to appear in a lineup before Chuck. It would be a crucial confrontation: either Chuck could positively identify Bennett as the assailant, or he could clear him of suspicion.

Not unexpectedly, Bennett's lawyer objected to the lineup and filed a formal request to prohibit it from taking place. But Superior Court Judge Constance Sweeney listened to arguments and rejected Bennett's plea: the lineup would take place, she said.

Bennett's lawyer appealed, but he was no more successful with that attempt than he had been in the lower court. On December 28 Supreme Judicial Court Judge Neil Lynch announced that he too felt the lineup was proper. A few hours later Chuck was hustled to downtown Boston for the critical event. Fresh from a bleak Christmas, a rail-thin Chuck, who had celebrated his thirtieth birthday ten days earlier, stood silently in a cheerless identification room in police headquarters while eight men, including Bennett, were paraded before him. None of the men spoke. After studying each member of the group, Chuck pointed at Bennett. "He looks most like the guy," he whispered.

Although Chuck left the headquarters building without talking to reporters, the *Globe* quoted an unidentified source as saying that Chuck's identification was "positive . . . absolutely crystal clear."

Whether that was indeed the case has not been revealed, but Bennett still was not indicted for the murders. Instead he was charged the next day with a second robbery. It was another lock on his cell door, but it wasn't the *big one*.

Unknown to the media and the public, major developments were occurring behind the scenes, developments that would soon send the Stuart case back to front pages and primetime newscasts around the world.

Apparently Michael was not the only person Matthew confided in about Chuck's alleged role in the shooting. He must have been talking it over as well with his girlfriend, Janet Monteforte.

Monteforte, in turn, went to her parents. Concerned that their daughter could somehow be tied in to what obviously was an extremely sordid situation, the Montefortes paid a Christmas Eve visit to their lawyer, John Perenyi, seeking advice. What Perenyi told them has not been disclosed, but judging from events that transpired in the following few days, he probably urged them to get together with the Stuarts to discuss a plan of action.

How much Chuck knew about this is uncertain. But since he was involved directly, it is unlikely that he was not at least aware of what was going on. In any case, Michael must have sensed that the lid was about to blow off; he must have realized that it would be futile to try to keep the secret much longer. He called a family meeting for January 1 to discuss the potentially volatile situation. It must have been a particularly upsetting period for him. Despite his careful silence, it seemed that Chuck was about to be revealed, under the best possible scenario, as a conspirator in the deaths of his wife and infant son. Apparently what concerned Michael and others in the family who knew about Chuck's alleged involvement was damage control, not the morality of their not having come forward with their knowledge sooner. The situation was beyond containment; the issue was how to deal with it so the least amount of harm would accrue. It was, in every sense, a most cynical and dispiriting view.

Chapter 9

January 1, 1990
Monday

New Year greetings must have rung hollow indeed in parts of Revere on the first day of 1990. It is doubtful that the good Catholic, sports-crazed Stuarts even watched with much enthusiasm as Notre Dame whipped up on Colorado in the Orange Bowl. They had much weightier things to deal with.

Where and when they met, and exactly who was there, has not been disclosed. Probably they met at Michael's house. In attendance, virtually for sure, were Michael, Mark, Matthew, Shelly, and Janet Monteforte, Matthew's girlfriend. Neysa, for reasons not disclosed, was not there. Neither, probably, was Chuck. It may have been the first time that Shelly and Mark were aware of Chuck's involvement, although unnamed Police Department sources have suggested otherwise.

From what developed later, it appears that Matthew expressed an inability to continue to keep suppressed what he knew about events in Mission Hill on the night of October 23 and the period immediately before that. Friends of Matthew's have said that when he came back from California in mid-December, he was a changed person. A boisterous, devil-may-care Irishman before he left, a chip off his old dad's block, he was sullen, nervous, and depressed when he returned. According to a friend, he was drinking more than usual and was prone to cry in his beer. Although most could not account for the change at the time, they were soon to learn the reason.

Matthew's decision, of course, may have been prompted by more than an attack of conscience. If he was tormented by the moral dilemma brought on by his knowledge, he would not have waited seventy-two days to decide to speak up. Later there would be speculation that his decision had been prompted by the fact that he could not stand by while his brother fingered Willie Bennett, who, while not exactly an innocent man, was at least apparently innocent of shooting Chuck and Carol, although even that has not yet been determined for certain, according to District Attorney Flanagan. Nevertheless it is improbable that Matthew, a true son of an Irish linen-white, blue-collar suburb, would have been overwhelmed with guilt about what was going to happen to a cop-hating black ex-con from the inner city. What seems more probable is that Monteforte told him that if he didn't do something, she would. Faced with an ultimatum like that, the lawyer Perenyi, who at some point took Matthew on as a client as well, may have advised him that he would fare better by going to the authorities himself.

Still, according to Perenyi, when Matthew announced his plans to the gathered siblings, they tried to talk him out of it. But apparently he was adamant. On January 3, the first convenient day after the holiday break, Matthew said he was going to the prosecutors to tell them what he knew about the incident.

From the meeting with his brothers, Matthew went to Reardon's Bar, the tavern owned by his cousin that was one of his favorite drinking places. He slumped over the bar, crying in his beer. Two friends who found him utterly dejected tried to cheer him up. Ever since he had come back from California, he had been subject to fits of deep depression, and they worried that he might be contemplating suicide.

"I've got to do it," he mumbled. "I've got to get it over with."

Certain now that their friend *was* talking about suicide, they told him that killing himself was no way out, no matter how bad things seemed.

Matthew shook his head. "You don't understand," he said. "That's not what I mean."

What do you mean? they asked.

He refused to answer. "When it happens you'll all know," he said cryptically. "The whole world will know."

In attempting to fathom Matthew's motives, there is another factor to consider as well. Although it was not a topic of frequent debate among the general public in Massachusetts, there still existed on the law books a statute known informally as "the blood relative law." Dating to 1784, the law was enacted at a time when the family was more important than the state. What it said, in essence, was that a person could not be prosecuted for harboring a blood relative who had committed a felony, not even for assisting said relative in concealing the crime. The law is generally interpreted to mean that a husband, wife, parent, grandparent, child, grandchild, *brother*, or *sister* cannot be prosecuted as an accessory after the fact. Apparently, in lawyer Perenyi's view, this was Matthew's legal lifeline. Even if he admitted involvement with Chuck, Perenyi apparently reckoned, Matthew could not be made to face charges.

But Matthew's decision may not even have been the major topic of discussion among the Stuart siblings. The major issue among them may have been how they were going to handle the inevitable disclosures. Since there is no evidence that the Stuarts approached the situation with anything but cynicism in the past, there is no reason to suspect they acted anything but cynically then. This was, unhappily, underlined a few days later when Shelly, Neysa, Michael, and Mark held a news conference with their flamboyant attorney, Richard Clayman, to announce their official position: They were not *legally* responsible for anything that had happened up until then. Moral responsibility, however, was something else.

January 2, 1990
Tuesday

Shelly, the oldest of the Stuart children, was particularly concerned about the impact the revelations could have on her father, Charles, and her stepmother, Dorothy, neither of whom was in good health. She felt the children were going to have to make a decision on what and how they were going to tell their parents. But no decision was made on January 1.

The next day, still not having heard anything from the family about breaking the news to Charles and Dorothy, Shelly called Michael at home to force the issue. Matthew's deadline was approaching; in twenty-four hours the whole world would know. Michael was on duty at the fire station, and his wife, Maria, called him there. Shelly needed to talk to him, she said: "It's an emergency."

Michael, perhaps forgetting that telephone calls to and from the fire station are recorded, called Shelly at her home.

"Hi," he said, sounding somewhat less than cheerful.

Shelly did not waste time with preliminaries. "We're all meeting here right now," she said. "We're going to Mom's."

Michael shilly-shallied. "Well, you know what it is. I can't leave here until I talk to the deputy."

"When will that be?" Shelly pressed.

"Well," Michael continued to dawdle, "he's on the road right now. I wouldn't even begin to tell you."

The answer didn't satisfy his sister. "Can't it be an emergency crisis at home?"

"I suppose I could say that," Michael conceded, "but—"

Shelly interrupted. "Say it, Mike, because it is."

Michael, resignedly: "What's going to happen?"

"We're going to tell Mom and Dad," Shelly said.

"What are you going to tell them?"

"We're going to tell them we know that Chuck was involved," Shelly said. "We're not going to say that he killed her."

"Wow," Michael replied.

"I know, Mike," Shelly said. "Get ready."

In response to a question from Michael, Shelly said the delegation to the elder Stuarts would consist of her and her husband, Steve, Janet Monteforte, Mark, and Matthew. "And Neysa's coming over," she added.

Michael sounded surprised. "Neysa doesn't know?"

That was right, Shelly responded, Neysa had not yet been told.

"Oh, Christ," said Michael. After giving the issue a few minutes of thought, he agreed that he would claim an emergency, leave the fire station, and join them. His wife, Maria, would want to go as well, he added.

"Tell her to come," Shelly said, "but you guys have to be here soon."

"Okay," Mike agreed.

"Like within ten minutes," Shelly responded, underlining the urgency.

Ringing off with Shelly, Mike dialed his wife and tersely explained the situation. He said he was going with them.

"Do they want it to be just the immediate family?" Maria asked.

"No, no," Michael replied, explaining that Steve Yandoli and Janet Monteforte would be there, too. Sighing, he said it would be up to her if she wanted to go with him. "Believe me," he added, "I don't want to be there."

"I'll go," Maria said. "Come and get me."

"All right," Michael said.

"I love you," said Maria.

"I love you, too," said Michael. "Bye."

What they told Charles and Dorothy has not been revealed. It also is not known if Chuck was there, but he likely was not. That Tuesday, January 2, was a busy day for him.

First he went to the bank and got a certified check for $10,000, delving into the $82,000 in Carol's life insurance that he had collected a few weeks earlier. Then he took the check and Carol's blue Toyota to a car dealer, where he used both the check and the trade-in value of the Toyota to buy a $22,277 new Nissan Maxima, which he drove off the lot. From there he went to a jewelry store in suburban Peabody and paid cash for a $250 gold brooch. Debbie Allen's twenty-third birthday was the next day, and there has been speculation that he bought the pin for her, whether he actually presented it to her or not. She denied she ever received it. From there he went to a second jewelry store and bought a pair of diamond earrings for $1,000. Apparently they were a gift for his mother.

What he did for the rest of the day is uncertain. Maybe he went drinking with friends. Maybe he rendezvoused with Debbie Allen. Maybe he went back to his house in Reading and played with the Labs, Max and Midnight. Maybe he went to his old church and prayed. Maybe he visited Carol's grave. What he did *not* do was go to the police, even though he almost surely knew that Matthew was going to the district attorney's office in twelve hours.

Whatever Chuck did, it may have been the last time he did it. In a little more than thirty-six hours he would be dead.

Chapter 10

January 3, 1990

Late in the afternoon, Matthew went to the district attorney's office, just as he had told his family he would. With him was his lawyer, John Perenyi, and his best friend, John "Jack" McMahon, a youth Matthew's age who made his living fixing vending machines. Prosecutors knew he was coming; Perenyi had paved the way for the visit. Although the lawyer had given the assistant district attorneys a synopsis of what Matthew had to say, they wanted to hear it from Matthew himself. The district attorney's office has refused to share its record of the meeting. But as best as can be determined, this is what was said:

A few weeks before the October 23 shooting, Chuck approached Matthew with an offer for a deal. Matthew was a little surprised by Chuck's friendliness because his brother had not been speaking to him for almost two years. Nevertheless he decided to listen. Although Chuck tended to be dictatorial, Matthew could not help but admire him. Chuck had gone farther than any of his other brothers—in fact, farther than anyone he knew. Most of the guys he had grown up with on the block, and their brothers, were still living in Revere, many of them still in their boyhood rooms in back of their parents' houses. If they worked at all, they had jobs that paid little better than minimum wage. But Chuck, without benefit of a college education—indeed without even a proper high school education—had landed a top job at one of the city's swankiest shops. He lived in a luxurious home in a well-to-do suburb, he dressed like a model in *GQ*, he traveled abroad, and he brought home more money in a year, not counting Carol's salary, than Matthew could earn in seven. Chuck, he figured, must know something he didn't know, and if his brother wanted his help and was willing to pay for it, the least he could do was listen.

Chuck told him, Matthew said, that he had a plan to rip off the insurance company for some sizable bucks, but he needed Matthew's help.

"Okay," Matthew replied. "Go ahead."

What we're going to do, Chuck said, was rob his house.

There was an incident in Matthew's past that may have made Chuck believe he would be receptive to that kind of approach. According to the *Globe*, about four years previously Matthew and a friend, both of whom had been drinking heavily, broke into an unoccupied house in Matthew's neighborhood. Just what they'd hoped to accomplish is uncertain because the house was empty and there was nothing to steal. Matthew regarded it as a hilarious prank, but the police didn't think it was so funny. They wanted to charge him with breaking and entering. But the owners were friends of the Stuarts', and they refused to press charges. Since then, although Matthew has been described as a youth who likes to party, he has never run into problems with the police. His previous employers told the *Globe* that he has an unmarred, even exemplary, work record.

Just how much of his alleged actual scheme Chuck revealed to Matthew is unclear. Newspaper reports, quoting unnamed sources within the police department, later claimed that Chuck planned to have Matthew break into the house, then he himself would kill his wife, Carol, and make it look as though she had been murdered by a burglar.

In any case, Matthew said he forced his way into his brother's Reading home, as agreed, and was collecting several specific objects that Chuck wanted to report stolen. But then Chuck and Carol came home earlier than expected, too soon for him to finish his job. He had to duck into a bathroom and then slip out while his brother and sister-in-law were in a different part of the house. If Chuck's plan had been to kill Carol, it was aborted. Matthew, needless to say, was unhappy with the turn of events. He had been promised $5,000 for his part in the plot. Working as a paint mixer, it would take him three months to make that.

Several weeks later, Matthew continued, Chuck came back to him and said he had another idea. Since Matthew has not spoken publicly on the issue himself, but only through his attorney, whom he would later fire, it is not altogether clear exactly what Chuck told him except that this latest scheme was more sophisticated than the previous one. Chuck hinted that it had something to do with his employer, Kakas & Sons. Matthew halfway assumed that Chuck was going to steal something from Kakas. Since this was a more elaborate plan and the stakes were higher, Matthew said Chuck told him, his services would be worth more. This time Chuck proposed to pay him $10,000. Matthew thought about it for about three seconds, then said, Hell, yes.

On Sunday, October 22, Chuck met Matthew near Brigham and Women's Hospital in Roxbury and took him on a long tour of the neighborhood. Finally Chuck picked a deserted spot deep within Mission Hill and told Matthew to memorize the location. Chuck said he would meet him at that spot the next night between eight-fifteen and eight-thirty, and he would have a package for him. Chuck told Matthew to leave open the window in the back of his car, and he, Chuck, would toss the package into Matthew's vehicle. Matthew then was to dispose of the package.

"Is that all?" Matthew asked.

"That's it," Chuck said.

The next night, October 23, Matthew said he was at the predetermined location when Chuck drove up. Neither one got out of their cars, but Chuck barked at Matthew to follow him to another location. When they got there Chuck tossed a small bundle into Matthew's car, ordered him to get rid of it, and drove away.

Until there is some official confirmation, this is where the story gets a little fuzzy. Although there is no known evidence that Matthew's friend, Jack McMahon, was with Matthew in Mission Hill, it seems more than a bit odd that Matthew would have sought McMahon out afterwards. In any case, we know McMahon was involved at the point that the gun and the jewels were thrown into the Pines River.

Presumably Chuck drove away from his meeting with Matthew and dialed 911. There has been speculation that he was particularly vague about his location in his conversation with Gary McLaughlin because he wanted to give Matthew plenty of time to get away before the police arrived. Considering the seriousness of Chuck's wound, this is difficult to believe. Matthew, nevertheless, is not qualified to speak on the subject because he wasn't there.

Matthew said he did not specifically notice Carol in the car. There may have been something in the front seat, he said, but he had no reason to think it was the body of his sister-in-law, who by then was breathing her last. Neither did he notice that Chuck was wounded or that he seemed to be in pain.

Matthew said once he was clear of the area he opened the bundle and saw that it contained a nickel-plated, snub-nosed revolver, a woman's purse, and some assorted jewelry and makeup. The sight of the gun threw him into a panic, he said. That is when he sought McMahon's help. Matthew and McMahon drove to an isolated area of Revere and walked out onto a railroad trestle, locally called the Dizzy Bridge, and tossed Chuck's bundle into the Pines River. First Matthew pocketed Carol's engagement ring because he thought Chuck might want to have that back, then he heaved the purse with its makeup and other jewelry into the cold, dark water. McMahon, exhibiting the form of a champion discus thrower, flung the gun.

Exhausted, but looking relieved, Matthew slumped on his chair. "That's it," he told the lawyers huddled around him. "That's the story."

"How do we know you're telling us the truth?" one of the prosecutors asked.

In reply, Matthew dug into his pocket and pulled out a small object, which he laid on the table. It was Carol's engagement ring, the 1.5-carat diamond glittering in the harsh overhead light.

If Matthew is ever required to tell his story in a courtroom where he would be subject to cross-examination, a good opposing attorney would have a field day. Just how much he knew and when he knew it is one area ripe for exploration. Even more so is what precisely happened on the night of October 23. At the time of transfer, how could Matthew *not* see Carol or notice that Chuck was wounded? Granted that Matthew's motive would be to make his story to prosecutors as self-serving as possible, the account still strains credibility. For things to have happened under this scenario, which later was outlined to reporters by Matthew's lawyer, Perenyi, Chuck would have to have shot Carol. Then he would have to have collected Carol's purse and jewelry, plus his own belongings, and gathered everything into a bundle. Then he would have to have driven to the vacant where the keys were found and toss them out. Then he would have to have shot himself and driven to his rendezvous with Matthew. From there, a badly wounded and bleeding Chuck, who would have been in considerable pain, would have to have gone to a second location to pass the bundle. And *then* he would have to have driven still farther while he spent thirteen minutes on the car phone with Gary McLaughlin.

Authorities, claiming it would be a violation of privacy to reveal such details, have not helped to clear up reservations many have about the shooting by releasing information about Chuck's and Carol's wounds. Would Chuck have been able to accomplish those tasks physically, considering that he was seriously gut shot? What about the forensic reports on Carol? Was she shot in the side of the head or the back of the head? If the wound was in the back, would the fatal shot have to have been fired from the backseat, given the trajectory of the entrance wound? If it were determined that she was shot from the backseat, did Chuck climb into the rear of the car on some pretense and then shoot her? Or was there indeed a gunman? If the wound was in the back of her head, could Carol have been shot while she had her head turned looking out the passenger window, rather than from the backseat? What was the angle of entry of Chuck's wound? Was the shot in such a location that he could not have fired it himself? Doctors at BCH said they had no reason to think that the wound was self-inflicted. If he did not shoot himself, who shot him?

* * *

Matthew's statement raised more questions than it answered. His story was detailed for the public by his lawyer, John Perenyi. Later Perenyi would also be criticized, as would Richard Clayman, the lawyer for the Stuart family, for giving away too much about their clients. Matthew may have felt that way about Perenyi in any case because several weeks later he fired him. Perenyi's replacement was well-known feminist rights lawyer Nancy Gertner, who promptly put a lid on *all* information about Matthew. If she was worried about charges being filed against him, she had good reason.

While Perenyi was still Matthew's lawyer he told reporters that Matthew had assurances from the prosecutors *before* he met with him that he was covered by the blood relative law and would not be charged as an accessory. Prosecutors, however, have denied making such promises. But even if it were determined that the blood relative law applied, would Matthew be covered?

During an appearance weeks later on the *People Are Talking* program on WBZ-TV, Boston's NBC affiliate, Harvard Law School's Alan Dershowitz pointed out that prosecution of Matthew, assuming he tried to claim immunity under the blood relative law, could in fact hinge on when it was determined that the actual crime was committed. That is, if the crime occurred when Carol was shot, then anything Matthew did afterward would be considered "after the fact," and he presumably could not be called to account as an accessory. However, if it is determined that the crime occurred when Carol died, rather than when she was shot, Matthew conceivably could be charged as an accessory *before* the fact, an accusation that may not be covered by the blood relative law.

Whatever the consequences will prove to be, Matthew's decision to tell his story, even if it was self-serving, set off a chain of events that still has Boston humming. The most serious consequence, though, at least as far as Chuck was concerned, was already in motion.

Chapter 11

Chuck knew—he *had* to know—that whatever Matthew told prosecutors, it did not bode well for him. He had not been able to convince his brother to keep quiet. Neither had his brothers and sister. The walls were closing in. Soon, he felt with certainty, the police would come looking for him. At the very least they would want to talk to him. More than likely they would haul him downtown and charge him. He had to do something. Even while Matthew was closeted with the assistant district attorneys in their office downtown, Chuck spun into motion.

Jumping into his new Nissan, he drove to his house in Reading. A neighbor later said he saw Chuck pull in, disappear inside, and a few minutes later leave again. Apparently he was en route to the office of his family's lawyer, John T. Dawley. Ironically Matthew had first turned to Dawley a week previously when he was looking for legal advice. Dawley turned him down, so Matthew went to his girlfriend's lawyer, John Perenyi. Dawley also turned Chuck down, telling him it would be a conflict of interest for him to represent him since he already represented his father and mother. Dawley did, however, scribble four names for Chuck, names of lawyers he said might be willing to take his case. Chuck pocketed the list and left.

Where he went from there is unknown, or at least it has not been disclosed. He did *not* go back to his house. Apparently he did not go to his parents' house, either. He could have gone to Michael's house. But he could have gone practically anywhere. Maybe he met with Debbie Allen. Maybe he just drove around. Whatever, his next known act was to check in at the Sheraton-Tara Hotel in Braintree, which is south of Boston. Chuck's house was in Reading, which is almost due north of Boston. His parents and his brothers lived in Revere, which is closer to Boston than Reading, but still to the north. To get to Braintree, he had to drive completely across the city. It's a long drive. Why he went to the Sheraton-Tara in Braintree is unknown. The sister hotel in Danvers would have been closer. There were hundreds of hotels he could have gone to. Maybe he felt an affinity with the hotel because he'd once worked at the other Sheraton-Tara when he had just graduated from the Voke.

10:00 P.M.

When Chuck checked in just before ten, he had been gone from his house in Reading for about six

hours. Except for the visit to Dawley, his movements during that time are unaccounted for. He
filled out the registration form and paid in advance
with a credit card. He had no luggage. Palming the
key to room 231, Chuck asked, as normally as if he
were a salesman with an early morning meeting,
for a wake-up call at 4:30 A.M., an ungodly hour to
be about unless there was someplace he had to be.
Or someplace he did *not* have to be, like loitering
around a hotel room while the police were busily
tracking him down. But that wasn't very likely.
There are just too many hotels in the Boston area
where he could have been. The fact that he left a
wake-up call at all, particularly at that hour, is
very odd considering what was to happen.

Chuck made one telephone call from his room,
but since it was to a Boston-area number it was not
recorded by the hotel's automatic equipment. The
charge reflected on his bill for the call was $1.50.
Apparently it was the only expense he charged to
his room.

January 4, 1990
2:00 A.M.

Some four hours after he checked in, Chuck left
the hotel and walked to a nearby all-night convenience store. The two clerks in the store, accustomed to eyeing middle-of-the-night customers
with a certain amount of skepticism because each
could be a potential holdup man, gave Chuck a
quick once-over. He appeared normal enough, they
said later, even jolly. He was grinning from ear to

ear, said Stephen Newton, which immediately made him suspicious. After all, who comes into a store in the middle of a freezing-cold night in such a good mood? They didn't have to worry, though; robbery was not on Chuck's agenda.

He browsed through the store, bought a soda and a snack, and, still smiling, paid for it with a small bill. As he left, he turned and cheerfully asked if the store remained open all night.

Newton's co-worker replied warily that it did.

"Okay," Chuck said, adding that he might come back if he got the munchies again.

Although there are no witnesses to confirm his movements, Chuck apparently returned to the hotel, polished off his early morning snack, emptied the change from his pockets into a hotel ashtray, and stretched out on the bed.

4:30 A.M.

Chuck's wake-up call came through as requested. He got up, put on his coat, and left the hotel, leaving behind the ashtray full of change and a colostomy bag, presumably a spare. Next to the telephone was the list of attorneys he had taken earlier from Dawley. He did not turn in his key. Whether he was simply forgetful or whether he planned to return to the room is unknown.

What happened in the next two and a half hours is still a mystery. There is little doubt that Chuck left the hotel immediately after his wake-up call, but where he went and what he did is speculation. It *is* known, however, that he changed clothes. The

clerks at the convenience store said he was wearing
a black pullover sweater and black slacks when he
strolled into the establishment at two A.M. But
when his body was recovered later from the Mystic
River, he was wearing blue jeans and a parka. Since
the clerk said he had no luggage when he checked
in, he must have gone somewhere to change. If he
thought the police were watching his house in
Reading, which indeed they were, and had been
since eleven o'clock the previous night, it is certain
he did not go there. Another possibility is that he
went to Michael's house in Revere. Debbie Allen
lived with her parents, and it is unlikely he went
banging on her door before dawn. But if he went to
Revere, what he did next is even more puzzling.

7:00 A.M.

While making his rounds, State Trooper Jerome
Cronin saw a new Nissan pulled over on the shoulder of the Revere-bound tier of the Tobin Bridge.
The emergency flashers were blinking; the hood
was propped open; the engine was running; and
the vehicle was empty. On the passenger seat was
a driver's license issued to Charles Stuart and a
handwritten note on Sheraton-Tara stationery. Although the police refused to divulge the text of the
note, they said it indicated that Chuck didn't have
the strength to continue, loved his family, and had
been through hell. . . . He added that the allegations
had drained him. Significantly, it was *not* a confession. Neither was it an explicit admission that he
intended to jump off the bridge.

Cronin ran a quick check on the license plate and confirmed that the vehicle was registered to Chuck. Fearing that it might be a smoke screen, the watch commander at the Commonwealth Avenue head-quarters ordered the detail at Logan International Airport to immediately begin checking outbound flights. So far they had no reports from anyone who said they saw a man jump off the bridge, and a staged suicide could be a clever hoax. A few min-utes later, though, they got a call from a man who said he thought he saw a body in the river. But police were taking no chances. They would keep watching the airport until Chuck's body was recov-ered.

Cronin peered over the bridge rail and shivered. The water was some 250 feet down, about as far as the ground would be if he were standing atop a twenty-five-story building. The river was gray and wind-whipped, not at all an inviting place. The air temperature was in the mid-thirties, and with a brisk wind blowing in off the ocean, the chill factor brought it down to the low teens.

Back at headquarters, playing the obvious, the watch commander called out the divers.

7:35 A.M.

Sergeant Leo Gerstel, the dive master on the local state police diving team, was snoring away at his home in suburban Melrose after working late the night before when the telephone jangled him awake. For Gerstel, early morning calls are almost routine. On the average, one person a month jumps into the Mystic River from the Tobin Bridge. Just a week before, they had recovered the body of a young sailor.

Of course, the divers only get the ones who make it to the water. Not infrequently, if the suicide jumps off the upper level, the winds blow him or her back into the bridge and the body lands on the lower level. Gerstel recalled one time when he was called out to investigate a reported jumper. As customary, the troopers searched the roadway first to see if they could find the spot from which the man was believed to have leaped. While they had their eyes down on the pavement and were examining the rail for scuff marks or scratches, they were startled by a loud, sickening thud. Swinging around, they saw the body of a man just a few feet away. Instead of vaulting over the rail by the roadway, the man had climbed up the superstructure before leaping. He almost fell on top of them.

Then again, it is not always a dead person that police recover from the river. Gerstel remembered one woman jumper who was alive when they pulled her from the water. She was taken to a hospital, where she underwent extensive treatment for her injuries. But as soon as she was released, she went straight back to the bridge and jumped again. The second time she succeeded in killing herself.

This morning, though, Gerstel's instincts told him the body would be in the river and the man would be dead. He proved to be right.

That morning, the water temperature in the Mystic River was 30 degrees Fahrenheit, only two degrees above that at which saltwater freezes. As he donned his dry suit, which would help insulate him from the cold, his face mask, air tank, and fins, Gerstel shivered slightly at the thought of how cold it was going to be when he leaped in. The amount of time he and his men could stay in the water would be limited. Besides the cold, another problem would be low visibility. The river is roiled by a strong current and tidal swirls. Once underwater, he knew, he and the others would not be able to see more than two feet in any direction.

He looked around at his crew. All told, there were five divers, and they would work in shifts of two for as long as they had air and didn't freeze. As usual in such situations, each diver positioned himself at one end of a seven-foot-long tow bar. The boat that they used as a diving platform would troll slowly across a predesignated grid, towing the bar and the two divers along the bottom, which was where they almost invariably found jumpers. Sometimes if the suicides were wearing particularly fluffy clothes, they would float slightly, but in most cases they sank like stones. Days later, when accumulated body gases gave them buoyancy, they would bob to the surface.

12:35 P.M.

Troopers Jerry DeCristofaro and Brian Menton, on the sixth dive of the morning, found Chuck Stuart. He was lying on the bottom twenty-five feet below the surface. There was no doubt that he was dead. The troopers maneuvered the body to the surface, where it was hauled aboard the boat and taken to shore for transfer to the morgue. As he helped pull him over the transom, Gerstel noted that Chuck had several abrasions on the side of his face, but he reckoned they resulted from his impact with the water. By the time he hit the Mystic River his body was traveling at about 120 miles per hour.

At the time he got word that Chuck's body had been pulled from the river, Carol's father Giusto DiMaiti, was at the pizza parlor that his son, Carl, had purchased a few years earlier. He was told that his son-in-law had jumped off the bridge because it looked as though police were closing in on him as the chief suspect in the murders of his daughter and infant grandson. A year earlier DiMaiti had undergone bypass surgery, and his heart had not yet fully recovered. "That can't be!" he screamed when he heard the news. "He was supposed to have dinner with us tomorrow night." Giusto said his wife, Evelyn, was preparing a special meal of lightly spiced chicken for Chuck because she knew that until his colon had healed from the bullet wound and the surgery, he had to watch his diet. With a look of confused disbelief, Giusto grabbed his chest and collapsed onto a chair. He was rushed to a hospital, but doctors said he had not suffered a heart attack. Apparently the news had, however, encouraged a spasm of angina.

How Chuck's siblings and his parents reacted is not known. They went into seclusion and refused to talk to reporters.

Friends of the couple and some other family members, however, were not quite as reticent.

Maureen Vadjic, a neighbor of Chuck and Carol's,

told the *Herald* she never would have believed such a circumstance would be possible. "Carol never spoke of any problems between them," she told reporter Harvey Dickson. "She was ecstatic about being pregnant. They were both very happy."

"It's unbelievable," said one unidentified member of Chuck's family. "Never in a million years would we think it. They seemed so happy."

Another unidentified family member suggested that Chuck may have leaped because he was despondent over the death of his wife and son.

One women who grew up with Carol, and still saw her frequently, said she and Carol often exchanged confidences. Never, said the woman, had Carol indicated that she and Chuck were having problems. "She would have told me if there were any problems, but she never even hinted at any."

Late afternoon

Another team of divers working the Pines River found the bundle containing Carol's handbag exactly where Matthew had said he had thrown it. According to "sources," the bundle contained Carol's jewelry and makeup. They did not mention Chuck's $600 watch. Whether it continues to be missing is a mystery.

Although the bundle of Carol's possessions was recovered relatively quickly, the gun proved elusive. When divers had to quit because of the cold and swirling tides, they still had not located the weapon. It would, in fact, not be found for four days and then only after Jack McMahon was persuaded to toss off the bridge, in a reenactment of his October 23 heave, an orange-painted metal object identical in weight to a snub-nosed, .38 caliber revolver. Divers who were waiting in the river followed the highly visible weight to the bottom and began searching there for the weapon. Almost immediately they found the gun half-buried in river silt. There were three expended rounds in the cylinder, which corresponded exactly with the number of shots Chuck said had been fired in the car. A ballistics report filed weeks later would confirm that the bullets that killed Carol and wounded Chuck had come from that gun.

Just before his office closed for the day, District Attorney Newman Flanagan issued a statement confirming that the body found in the Mystic River that morning was that of Chuck Stuart. The cause of death was listed as drowning. It added, almost gratuitously, that a "spent bullet" had been recovered from Chuck's abdomen during the autopsy. This was the bullet from the October 23 gunshot. Hospital authorities had been so secretive about Chuck's condition and treatment that they had never mentioned it had never been removed.

The DA had one other thing to say as well, something that would prove as explosive as the fact that Chuck was dead and his brother Matthew was somehow involved in the crime. The statements from Matthew and Chuck's other siblings, Flanagan said, "clearly exculpated Willie Bennett and clearly inculpated Charles Stuart in the murder of his wife and infant son." But in criminal investigations, nothing is forever. Weeks later Flanagan would reveal an apparent change of heart.

Again, the known facts raise numerous questions. Just about everybody assumes that Chuck committed suicide. Although that is likely the case, there are enough variables to keep it from being a certainty. No one saw him jump. His note did not explicitly say he was going to commit suicide. His note was not a confession. Even if he had been arrested, he might not have been convicted. On the basis of Matthew's story, Chuck became a very good suspect, but only a suspect. He did not appear to be the suicidal type, and several things in his behavior mitigated against such an act. Why did he buy a new car only hours earlier? Why did he feel it necessary to pay for a large chunk of the purchase price with a cashier's check? Why did he go to the Sheraton-Tara? Why did he still have his room key? Whom did he call? Where was he for the five or six hours the previous evening and the two and a half hours that morning? Where did he change clothes, provided of course that the convenience store clerks had correctly identified their early morning customer? What happened to the clothes he had on? If he was contemplating suicide, why did he appear cheerful at two A.M.? Was he on drugs? Why did he leave a wake-up call? How many potential suicides leave wake-up calls because they are afraid they will oversleep their date with death? In the following days it became a great sport for psychologists and psychiatrists to make a postmortem diagnosis of Chuck Stuart's mental state. The general consensus was that he was at best a narcissist, at worst a sociopath. But neither type is particularly suicidal, impulsive, or depressed in personality. On the contrary, psychopaths and narcissists are deliberate and rational; they believe they can charm their way out of any tight corner.

Also very important, why did Chuck leave his car on the Revere-bound tier of the Tobin Bridge? If he had been to Revere to change clothes, he would have to have crossed the Tobin Bridge on the Boston-bound upper tier to leave the community, then turned around and gone *back* across the bridge on the lower tier, where his car was found. If he had been intent on jumping, why didn't he jump from the Boston-bound tier, which is considerably higher anyway?

There was one other extremely puzzling thing. In their efforts to get comments from persons involved with the case, reporters interviewed Carol's uncle, Mario DiMaiti. He was quoted in the Quincy *Patriot Ledger* as saying the DiMaiti family may have taken the situation into its own hands if the members had suspected Chuck murdered Carol. "We said we'd kill him ourselves if he had anything to do with Carol's killing," Mario told Scott Allen.

Chapter 12

Predictably, headlines the morning after Chuck's body was found bellowed his guilt. The *Globe*, on the top of page one, across all six of its extra-wide columns, printed the headline STUART DIES IN JUMP OFF TOBIN BRIDGE AFTER POLICE ARE TOLD HE KILLED HIS WIFE. It was a great headline, but it was wrong or, at best, premature. It left no room for doubt that Chuck killed himself, and it certified that he had killed Carol. What the *Globe* did was what no newspaper should ever do: it turned an assumption, actually two assumptions, into fact. This marked the beginning of a sad saga of trial by newspaper.

The accompanying text, by writers Kevin Cullen, Sean Murphy, and Mike Barnicle, gave the headline added strength. "Charles M. Stuart killed himself yesterday," it said, "hours after his brother told police Stuart had planned and executed the robbery and shooting of his pregnant wife and then shot himself to cover up one of the most heinous crimes in recent history, police said." This compounded the headline writer's error. Barring the existence of at least one witness who actually saw Chuck alone on the bridge, someone who watched him climb over the rail and leap, the assertion that he did so is only speculation. The assumption becomes even shakier considering the ambiguous language in the note found in his car.

The story was more correct than the headline regarding Chuck's role in Carol's shooting. The headline implied that Matthew had told police that Chuck killed Carol. Until, and if, a transcript of Matthew's statement is divulged and additional information is disclosed, that statement is incorrect. According to his lawyer, Matthew did *not* see Chuck shoot Carol. In fact, he said he did not see Carol at all. And as far as what Matthew saw on the night of October 23, unless someone else was with Matthew to support his claims, there is only Matthew's word since neither Chuck nor Carol can contradict him. Is it unlikely that things occurred differently from the way Matthew says they did? Maybe, but this has been a very unusual story. Matthew did not do his case any good by waiting seventy-two days to tell his side. But by readily accepting Matthew's story, the *Globe* seemed to be making the same error it made in readily accepting Chuck's. Of course, the *Herald* acted the same way. And so did everyone else.

One of the really interesting things about the

Globe story, however, was that the two words in the first paragraph, "police said," are the closest the text comes to official attribution. Euphemisms are scattered throughout the story—"sources familiar with the investigation" . . . "authorities" . . . "investigators" . . . "sources" . . . "detectives"—but there are no solid quotes. The only police official quoted by name anywhere in the lengthy *Globe* story is Reading Detective David Saunders, who said police did indeed go to Chuck's house on the night of January 3.

The *Herald* coverage was almost identical. Its headline, which took up most of the right side of the tabloid's front page, read simply, HE DID IT FOR CASH. The subhead read: "Probers Point to Insurance Policy." The *Herald* also branded Chuck a suicide, and it did no better than the *Globe* in attributing its information. No names were mentioned, nor would they be in coming weeks.

Both papers also went out of their way to establish a motive: the *Herald* in its front-page headline, the *Globe* deeper into its story. The only substantiation for the *Herald*'s claim, however, came in the first paragraph in a phrase that said his motive was to "collect on her lucrative life insurance policy."

The *Globe* was more verbose. It said: "Authorities theorize Stuart killed his wife in order to collect several insurance policies he held on her totaling a half million dollars or more."

Eventually the newspapers would decide that Chuck had taken out policies on Carol's life totaling almost $1 million. But in the absence of proof, that figure was speculative. If police did, indeed, have evidence of such policies, they did not share the details with the media.

Late that afternoon the phone rang in the office of District Attorney Flanagan. The caller was a male, asking to speak to the assistant district attorney handling the Stuart case. "I have some information that you may be interested in," the voice said.

The caller was Jay Kakas, co-owner of Kakas & Sons furriers, where Chuck had worked for eight years. Kakas, apparently as shaken as everyone else by the recent turn of events, apologized for not calling sooner with the information he had to divulge.

"What is it?" the ADA asked impatiently.

"It's about the gun," Kakas said. "I think it's ours."

Kakas said the store had purchased a pistol long ago as a protection against robbery. At the time, he said, he had applied for and received a permit for the weapon. However, after the store hired an armed security firm to take over such duties, Kakas had stuck the gun in the store's safe and forgotten about it. That had been at least ten years before, and the permit had long ago expired.

"Where's the gun now?" the ADA wanted to know.

"I don't know," Kakas replied. "It's missing. It's been stolen."

"What kind of gun was it?"

"It was a snub-nosed, thirty-eight-caliber pistol," Kakas said.

"Was it nickel-plated?"

"Yes," replied the furrier.

"Did Charles Stuart have access to the safe? To the gun?"

"Of course," said Kakas. "He was my general manager."

Why it had taken Kakas more than two months to realize there might be a connection between the pistol kept in the shop's safe and the shooting incident, especially when a description of the weapon allegedly used in the assault was so widely publicized, was never explained satisfactorily. Kakas said he simply had forgotten about the pistol, and the possibility that it could have been the weapon used to kill Carol did not occur to him until after Chuck's apparent suicide.

According to the *Herald*, FBI tests on the weapon, which was recovered from the Pines River a few days after Kakas's telephone call, determined that the saltwater-corroded pistol was indeed the same weapon that Kakas had registered a decade before. The newspaper added that tests also determined that the weapon was the one used to fire the bullets that killed Carol and wounded Chuck. However, there was room for doubt because the official report had not yet been made public.

According to the *Globe*, a reporter from the newspaper had asked Jay Kakas soon after the shooting if Chuck owned a pistol. Kakas said no. Did he carry a store-owned weapon in the van when he was on company business? Kakas replied in the negative. Did you keep a pistol in the store? "No," Kakas said.

* * *

The first reports on the day after Chuck's death set the tone for the media coverage in forthcoming weeks. It was, in a word, hysterical. Significantly, the early reports delineated several things that would erroneously, or prematurely, be treated as givens by practically every news organization covering the story. And that would be virtually every news organization of any size in the country. In one week the Stuart story would be on the covers of *Newsweek*, *Time*, and *People* magazines, a virtually unheard-of situation. Devotees of *Time* and *Newsweek* are not necessarily avid readers of *People*, but fascination with the Stuart saga was so far-reaching that everyone felt compelled to get in on the act. Newspapers from Boston to Bakersfield devoted as much space to the case as if it were a local story. For a while, *The New York Times* ran a story almost every day. Also giving it heavy play, among others, were the *Los Angeles Times*, *The Washington Post*, and hundreds of smaller newspapers, not to mention United Press International, the Associated Press, and the British news agency, Reuters.

The New York Times, incidentally, was not free from error in its initial break. Its story on January 5 also unqualifiedly labeled Chuck a suicide in its headline, although the story attributed the assertion to "authorities," which was correct. The *Times* relied heavily on Flanagan for its attribution, and that tended to give its story more credibility. But the newspaper made a major mistake when it incorrectly stated that the bullets that killed Carol and wounded Chuck came from different guns. The error was corrected in later stories.

Television was, perhaps, even more fascinated

with the case. On the night Chuck's body was found, local stations, in the words of the *Herald*'s Monica Collins, "went wall-to-wall with coverage." All three major network affiliates broadcast District Attorney Flanagan's news conference live. And WNEV-TV, the city's CBS affiliate, canned the popular *Wheel of Fortune* to show a quickly assembled special on developments in the case. WNEV also scored a coup with an interview with Matthew's lawyer, John Perenyi. Commenting on that interview, Collins wrote: "Perenyi—his eyes skittering away from the camera, his answers both pointed and vague—left the indelible impression that the Stuarts were a family in turmoil and that Charles Stuart was guilty."

The story also was big on the networks. In addition to the regular news broadcasts on ABC, NBC, CBS, and CNN, the Stuart saga was featured in special programs. *Entertainment Tonight*, the *Today* show, *Nightline*, *Donahue*, *Morton Downey, Jr.*, and *Geraldo* all broadcast segments on the case. But it was in Boston, of course, that the coverage was pervasive. It was in the newspapers, on the radio, and on TV, and it was the major topic of conversation around hundreds of thousands of water coolers and private homes.

As usual, the coverage ran from the tasteful, such as that on WGBH, Boston's famed public television station, to the tasteless, such as the radio talk show host who invited callers to share the latest "Chuck jokes."

There was, however, no humor in the social, moral, and political upheaval that resulted from Matthew's admissions and Chuck's death. Literally overnight, millions of people around the country and around the world had to adjust to a 180-degree attitude flip. From everything that had been developed up until then, the Stuart case was the epitome of the dangers always present in an urban society. It showed what could happen to an innocent young white couple fro suburbia when they dared to venture into an inner-city mixed-race neighborhood, one where drug use was prevalent and crime was ubiquitous. Nowhere, naturally, was this more evident than in Boston itself. What continues to be shocking about the case, however, is the strident tone adopted by the Boston media. Until January 4 they were aggressively pushing the point of view that Chuck and Carol were victims and the villain was a black man. The implication was heavy that Willie Bennett was the man.

Then, within twenty-four hours, the view changed completely. Willie Bennett was innocent and Chuck was the fiendish perpetrator, the conscienceless degenerate who killed his pregnant wife and, indirectly, his infant son. His motive: money. What members of the media overlooked in their competitive zeal, in their blatant self-righteousness, was that neither man had proved to be what they said he was; that neither had been judged guilty except in their reports. Before January 3, when Matthew went to the authorities, Willie Bennett was regarded as the chief suspect, but he had not been convicted. After January 3 Chuck Stuart became the chief suspect. He had not been convicted, except in the media, which continued to label him a suicide and a murderer. One example of the media reaction was an article by Mike Barnicle, a *Globe* columnist who seems to want to be regarded as Boston's answer to Jimmy Breslin. A few days after Chuck's body was found, he wrote a memorable column that began: "When Charles Stuart, the lying murderer who will be forever infamous, jumped to his death last week . . ."

Barnicle, in fact, would become the *Globe*'s star in its Stuart case coverage. With a brother who is a detective for the city police, Barnicle's tips formed the basis for much of the *Globe*'s coverage. For a time, at least, the line between opinion and unbiased reporting effectively disappeared.

Boston officials cannot be held blameless, either. By adopting a policy of strict silence, they aggravated and abetted the situation. One of the most remarkable things about the Stuart case has been the incredibly widespread policy of official silence. Virtually every official from doctors at the hospital to Mayor Flynn buried his head and refused to speak on the record, hiding instead behind time-honored claims such as the sanctity of medical records and the inability to comment on an on-going investigation. That left reporters with no other choice but to go with unidentified sources and rumor. Seldom, in any case of such magnitude and wide public interest, has there been as blatant an effort to suppress pertinent information.

But if official Boston was keeping a low profile, Willie Bennett certainly was not. As soon as Chuck's death was announced, Robert George, Bennett's lawyer of the moment, issued a hyperbolic statement, purportedly drafted by Bennett (who still has not allowed his voice to be heard publicly), bitterly criticizing police and prosecutors.

"It is a shame that it took the suicide of the real killer this morning to open people's eyes to the fact that I am innocent and have always been," the statement read. "Yet nothing anyone can say or do will ever repair the terrible damage which has been caused to myself and my loved ones. My life . . . has been ruined."

It took a lot of courage for Bennett to say that—the statement that his "life had been ruined" was an especially pointed dig at Boston officials—coming as it did from a man who has averaged 1.6 arrests a year for every year of his life, including his childhood and the years he spent in prison.

George, also unable to restrain himself, elaborated upon the comments attributed to Bennett. "They have ruined somebody's life, and someone has to take responsibility for it," he said, adding that he was expecting the grand jury to indict his client that week for the murders of Carol and Christopher Stuart. "The prosecution twisted and adjusted the focus of the investigation," he said. "They pushed people to testify, so they heard only bits and pieces of information. No amount of bobbing and weaving on the issues in this case can hide the fact that Bennett was a scapegoat and the prosecutors destroyed his life."

The *Globe* story also contained quotes from members of Bennett's family, all of which echoed the anger expressed by George and his client.

"There's white man's justice and black man's justice," Bennett's brother, Ronald, was quoted as saying. "We were trying to tell you the first time, he didn't do it," said Bennett's sister Diane, one of the sisters who gave Bennett a contradictory alibi when he was arrested in November.

The *Herald* story covered the major points in George's news conference but couldn't resist taking an editorial slap at police (and patting itself on the back) at the same time. Deep in the news story about George and Bennett were these two puzzling paragraphs:

> On three occasions during the two weeks following the Stuart shootings, a *Herald* reporter urged Assistant District Attorney Francis O'Meara to probe the possibility that Charles Stuart was involved in the shootings, citing numerous suspicious comments and actions by Stuart during his 15-minute-long [sic] telephone conversation with State Police.
>
> In that tape-recorded conversation, Stuart appeared to be resisting the police dispatcher's efforts to locate him by refusing to identify signs or other landmarks in the area. And despite the dispatcher's urgings, Stuart refused to call out to passersby for help, even though Stuart was driving along heavily traveled Tremont St. for several minutes.

The whole world, it seemed, was caught up in the emotionalism that Chuck's death and Matthew's admissions had spurred. As choleric as George and Bennett were, they were not the only ones to vent their outrage at the turn of events. Civil rights advocates across the city also lambasted everyone in sight.

Chapter 13

Chief among those taking police and prosecutors to task for the way they had handled the case was Bruce Bolling, a dapper, articulate city councilman from Roxbury, who, until the latest developments occurred, had been a backer of Flynn's stop-and-search policy—in fact had been active in a group that set up an anticrime hotline called Drop-A-Dime. The search technique did not originate with Chuck's and Carol's shootings. It had begun the previous spring after an outbreak of gang- and drug-related violence. Its professed goal was to make the inner-city neighborhoods safer, but what it did was make a lot of the residents of those neighborhoods very angry indeed. By October 23 the policy was already highly controversial. The previous August a judge had dismissed charges of carrying a gun against a reputed gang member who was arrested during a search, calling the police stop-and-search tactic unconstitutional. Then the judge went one step further and asked the state attorney general, James Shannon, to review the policy. On October 15, a little more than a week before the Stuart shooting, Shannon ruled in favor of the police. He had determined, he said, that there was no *official* policy to search on sight, so there was nothing he could do.

About the same time, a furor arose when an unarmed man was shot by police who had stopped him and planned to search him during a sweep in Franklin Hill, another housing project. Following that incident, the black leadership split on the efficacy of the program, and the weekly *Boston Phoenix* reported that neighborhood residents were divided almost equally on whether the program should continue or be dropped. When it took on renewed vigor after the Stuart shooting, the atmosphere was already highly charged. Police, according to critics, did not help ease the tension by their excessive belligerence in trying to find the man Chuck said had shot him and his wife. According to the *Phoenix*, which quoted critics of the program, officers adopted a crude and pointed aggressiveness, stopping everyone in sight and repeating the question, "Okay, nigger, who pulled the trigger?"

During the debate and the sweeps through Mission Hill, Bolling and others who had supported the search policy remained silent. But when Chuck died, they exploded. On the day after Chuck's body was recovered, Bolling spoke his mind. "This case has stirred racial fears not only in Boston, but nationally," he said angrily. "A whole community and, in some cases, a whole race has been maligned." He called for apologies "across the board," citing specifically Mayor Flynn, Police Commissioner Roache, District Attorney Flanagan, and Governor Dukakis. They need, he said, to admit a "major mistake has been made" in allowing the public to believe that a black man had killed Carol and Christopher.

Another among the more vocal critics was Louis Elisa, president of the local chapter of the NAACP, who accused Flynn of instigating "national hysteria" by ordering police sweeps in Mission Hill the previous autumn. He also demanded that the mayor apologize.

The Reverend Charles Stith, a moderate and president of the Organization for a New Equality, was easier on Flynn than the others, arguing that the mayor should not be made the "fall guy" in the drama. "From where I sit," Stith said, "the media is as culpable as anybody in this. It was the classic representation of black people as either the victims or vermin."

These expressions from Stith, Elisa, Bolling, and others were only the beginning of thousands of words that would be printed and broadcast about the issue. Seemingly desperate to excuse their earlier apparent failure to be skeptical enough, the Boston media went overboard in trying to compensate for what it perceived to be previous poor judgment. Anyone who wanted to yell racism was given a platform, not only in Boston, but in New York, Washington, and around the country. The Stuart case was exploding on the national scene with a fervor that made the coverage in October seem minuscule. It was too good a case for the media *not* to pursue enthusiastically, incorporating, as it did, questions about race, uxoricide, infanticide, suicide, psychosis, wife abuse, police and prosecutor incompetence, sibling loyalty, official silence, and old-fashioned greed.

The immediate response in Boston's black community to Chuck's death was outrage, a vehement outpouring of anger by blacks who felt they had once again been subjected to abuse and discrimination by a white power structure that was looking for a convenient scapegoat. It had become, in essence, a reverse image of the Tawana Brawley case in New York. In that incident, a black teenaged girl claimed she was kidnapped, raped, tortured, and held prisoner by a group of white men, some of whom were wearing law enforcement badges. Although there are some diehards who still argue that Brawley spoke the truth, a grand jury proclaimed her claims a hoax, and she has generally, and roundly, been discredited.

Some of the arguments put forth by those who claimed that racism guided the early investigation in the Stuart case were reasoned and well put. Others were not. In a sense those who were now so quick to jump on the racist bandwagon were being just as exploitative as those, like Dukakis and Attorney General Shannon, who had earlier used the shootings to try to further their own political ends.

Anthony Walton, who lives in Portland, Maine, and writes frequently on racial issues, appeared on *The New York Times* op-ed page with a column that said the Stuart case should be used as an example for the nation because all Americans have a lot to learn about racism. "What kind of country is this, what kind of community of common ground do we have, when we are so willing to believe the worst about each other?" Walton wrote. "What if Charles Stuart hadn't cracked? How would we, black and white, have acted? What if the perpetrator *had* been black, but not Willie Bennett, the accused? Why was it so powerful that the killer was or was not black? What if the accused had been white?"

Derrick Bell, who teaches civil rights law at Harvard, also expressed his views for the *Times*, arguing that many Americans were willing to accept Chuck's story because it reinforced racial stereotypes. "The fear of black crime is, of course, not all based on myth," he wrote. "Black men in Boston, as in most urban areas, commit a disproportionately large percentage of all violent crime. Mr. Stuart's hoax was plausible because black crime is real." But that reality, he said, went deeper than crime itself; it penetrated to the roots of American society and had its origin in economics and class. "Charles Stuart was not burdened by the racial prejudice that discourages and ultimately destroys so many African Americans. He was a white man who, from the perspective of poor blacks, had everything that so many of them turn to crime to get. The nature of his crime makes Mr. Stuart a special case, but his bold effort to shift the blame for his deed is an American tradition that virtually defines the evil that is racism."

William Raspberry, a syndicated columnist based in Washington, wrote in the *Post* on January 8 that the Stuart case made him angry, but he was not sure whom to be angry at. "The revelation that the police no longer believe a black man was responsible for the double shooting was greeted with one part relief and ninety-nine parts outrage. I'm still outraged," he wrote, "that Stuart, whatever his desperate reasons, fingered a black man for the murderous deed. Black America is still angry, and our anger is not moderated—may even be intensified by—the fact that we aren't quite sure where to direct it." At whom should he focus his anger? he asked. "At Stuart, of course, but that is an empty passion. After all, he's dead, and at his own hand. At white America for believing his lie? But we believed it, too. At the Boston police? Well, yes, we didn't like their stop-and-search tactic, but we would hardly have been less angry if they had gone looking for their black 'suspect' with utmost courtesy and professionalism."

Fellow Washington columnist Richard Cohen, writing in the *Post* three days later, agreed that black outrage was justified to a certain extent. If it had been a black couple shot by a white man, the reaction probably would have been quite different. But he, like Bell in the *Times*, said that black crime could not be overlooked. "Too many blacks are focused entirely on racism, not noticing, it seems, that the criminals who are bopping them over the head are black themselves. So credit Charles Stuart with something. He knew his country. When he wanted to frame someone for his wife's murder, he chose a whole category—young black men. We all—blacks and whites—believed his story until the lie was exposed. Then the bickering resumed, turning the tragedy of murder into an even greater one. If we can't agree a problem exists, we can't even start to agree on a solution."

Some newspapers, the *Boston Herald* and *USA*

Today, for example, ran columns side by side giving opposing advocates the chance to express their views.

Julianne Malveaux, a California writer, economist, and former resident of Boston, argued in *USA Today* that Chuck, Mayor Flynn, and the *Globe* were members of a list of current racists that included Ronald Reagan, Lee Atwater, and President Bush. "This case fans every racial fire there is, and highlights every inequality." What particularly galled her, she said, was that "the finger-pointing of any white man can make an entire black community suspect."

Opposing her was John Lofton, a former New England newspaper editor now living in Laurel, Maryland. "Despite the repetition of the charge, ad nauseam, by some, there was no 'stereotyping of blacks' in the murder of Carol Stuart and her unborn baby. In fact, if any racial stereotyping has occurred, it could be argued that it was and is by those who charge 'racism!' every time a white person accuses a black of anything. But such charges are also a hoax."

In the *Herald*, Boston writer Margaret Doris argued to support charges of racism, claiming that Chuck pandered to stereotypes by telling the story he did to police. "We may never know if Charles Stuart shot his wife and unborn child, or if he was covering for the person who did. What we do know is that he intentionally created a story about that night, a story that had at its heart the cultural myth of the black bogeyman. As long as there are fine white boys who know how to sell a story," she wrote, "there will always be an audience for the bogeyman."

Presenting a contrary view for the *Herald* was columnist Don Feder, who claimed that the impetus for the current problems resulting from the Stuart case goes back more than a quarter of a century, that the pigeons of the 1960s are now coming home to roost. "The racialization of American justice started with the black-power movement," he said. "Any black charged with a crime automatically was reckoned innocent, the victim of injustice. Every criminal case was turned into an us-against-them contest." The Stuart investigation, he argued, was not about racism. "The only sinister aspect of the affair is the demand that we now grovel before the guilt-mongers."

But most of the statements in Boston tended toward the inflammatory. A man named Tony Van Der Meer organized a boycott against the *Globe* and the *Herald*. Willie Bennett's seventeen-year-old daughter, Nicole, said her father should "sue every one of you." Some black leaders, feeling an apology would be insufficient, called for the resignation of Flynn and his police commissioner, Mickey Roache. The Reverend Graylan Ellis-Hagler, pastor of Roxbury's Church of the United Community, accused Flynn, Flanagan, Dukakis, and the news media of contributing to a "lynch-mob mentality." And Bolling, apparently carried away with his own oratory, threatened unspecified but unpleasant action. "We are not going to be trodden on anymore. . . . We are going to dictate what the city is going to do. I have had enough! This community has had enough! We collectively are going to tell you what is good for us!"

Some were even more strident. A Roxbury community activist named Sadiki Kambon accused Flynn of ordering "a South Africa–style attack" when he sent police into Mission Hill in the hours after the shooting. He said he would not accept an apology from Flynn even if one were forthcoming. "We will not let this message die," he said.

Apparently seeking to bring reason back to a situation that appeared to be steamrolling out of control, a group of more moderate blacks suggested that a special legislative committee be formed to investigate how the city's institutions reacted and how the police response could have been more effective and less intrusive. It was a breath of fresh air in a climate that tended toward the frantic.

Flynn, seemingly anxious to mend fences, especially with a probable race for governor on his mind, visited Willie Bennett's family the night Chuck's body was hauled from the Mystic River. But it only made the Bennetts and many of the black activists angrier. "The mayor came and spent one hot second in my mother's home," said Willie Bennett's brother, Ronald. "Then he flew out the door. My mother offered him a chair to sit in, but he didn't want to sit down. He acted like my mother's house wasn't good enough for him."

While the fight raged, Flynn tried to keep a low profile. In fact, it may have been too low. On January 15, eleven days after Chuck's body was recovered, Flynn was one of the speakers at a memorial breakfast honoring the late Dr. Martin Luther King, Jr. Addressing the crowd of about 2,500 people, Flynn focused on a community investment plan involving a bankers association and the minority community. He did not mention the Stuart case. The fact that he did not angered many blacks anew. "It seems his advisers are telling him, 'If you act like it doesn't exist, it's going to go away.' But it's not going to go away," NAACP director Elisa said indignantly. Dukakis was another speaker at the gathering, and he did not address the Stuart case, either, but his failure to do so did not incur the wrath that Flynn's omission did.

The racism aspect of the story, however, was only one of several that was developing simultaneously. Events were popping so fast that the news media were having trouble keeping up with them. The result was the dissemination of reports covering subjects that ranged from the mundane to the exotic. Some of the news reports complemented each other, dovetailing one into the other to bring a specific incident into sharper focus. Some of them were diverse, coming straight out of left field. Some of them apparently were right. Some of them were obviously wrong. The main thing they had in common was that in virtually every one of them, specifics of the investigation were attributed to unidentified sources. It was an example of massive media coverage being directed by rumor; film was shown, recordings were broadcast, thousands of words were printed, but almost every substantive investigatory issue was handled without confirmation— there was simply no way of nailing it down. This made it possible for the *Globe* and the *Herald* to publish stories that were categorically denied, stories that may never have been published in the first place if Boston authorities had been willing to address the issues in an on-the-record basis. The result was confusion. If the media can be accused of stooping to disseminate rumor, then officials also can be accused of neglecting their responsibilities in separating fact from fiction.

Crucial to an interpretation of what had happened and why is an acknowledgment that a judgment cannot be based solely on the accuracy of news reports. Some of the material that was printed and broadcast was spot on, but much was woefully incomplete. Time and again many of the important questions never got answered, and although the secondary questions were answered correctly, they meant little without the answer to a primary question to bring it all into focus. In short, more issues were raised than resolved.

Some of those answers may come in time. Some may never come. In the days immediately following Chuck's death there were pitiably few verities. There was no question that Chuck was dead. There was no question that his brother Matthew was involved in the aftermath of the October 23 shooting. There was no question that a plot of some kind existed. Who the plotters were, what the plot was, how it was carried out, what the plotters' roles were, and what were the ultimate objectives—all were questions without answers. Despite the outrage of the black community, Flanagan has now backed off his early claim that Willie Bennett was no longer a suspect.

There were big gaps in the narrative. And while the public waited for someone to fill them in, the media was forced to scavenge voraciously, writing

articles and filing stand-uppers that were based
mainly on speculation. These were safe stories,
because in such cases any one reporter's story was
as good as anyone else's.

On the day after Chuck's body was recovered and
for a long time to come, only one thing would
remain certain: that his death and Matthew's visit
to the authorities had not closed the Stuart file. In
the days ahead the file just got thicker; the situation got more bizarre by the hour.

Chapter 14

Throughout metro Boston, it seemed, the reaction to these new developments was universal: shock and disbelief. The public, unaware that Matthew was going to speak to the authorities, still thought of Chuck as a brave survivor, a heroic victim of inner-city crime. The initial shock, however, quickly gave way to widespread anger. People who had followed developments in the case avidly through the media, who had shed tears when they heard Chuck's eulogy for his dead wife, who had shed more tears when the infant Christopher died, who suffered when news of Chuck's second operation was disseminated, felt frustrated and cheated. One Boston psychologist, who had no direct connection to the case, said that when his clients came to see him about their own problems, they were much more interested in spending their expensive and valuable time talking about how outraged they were by Chuck's apparent deception.

The people of Boston, it appeared, felt they had a stake in Chuck's future, and when it looked as though everything he said had been a lie, they were left with terrible feelings of resentment and pain. They were looking for someone to tell them not just what had happened, but why. They hungered for an explanation of how such a clean-cut family man like Chuck—and he had certainly been portrayed in that fashion by the media up till then—could have done what the media was *now* saying he did. For the Boston media, the explanation was simple: Chuck was an archfiend, the worst kind of monster, and the kind that was hardest to detect. He was, as the media were later to classify him, a sociopath, one of the tribe whose infamous members included John Wayne Gacy, Ted Bundy, and Jeffrey McDonald.

The *Herald* was the first to promote this new and interesting angle. Chuck's body had no sooner been pulled from the water than reporter Susan Brink rang Jack Levin, a sociologist at Northeastern University who has attained a considerable amount of fame from books and appearances on talk shows. She asked for an instant psychological diagnosis. Most experts, when called by a reporter begging for a quote, feel obligated to say *something*. Levin, not surprisingly, complied. Chuck, he said, referring to the call to state police, "playacted that dramatic sequence of events over the telephone." From that moment on, Levin asserted, Chuck had one goal in mind: fool the police and the public.

Without ever actually labeling Chuck a sociopath

Carol and Chuck Stuart seemed like the perfect couple.
(AP/Wide World Photos)

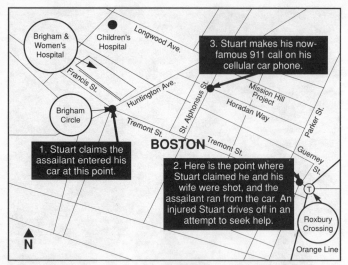

Map labels:

Brigham & Women's Hospital

Children's Hospital

Longwood Ave.

Francis St.

Brigham Circle

Huntington Ave.

Tremont St.

BOSTON

Tremont St.

St. Alphonsus St.

Mission Hill Project

Horadan Way

Parker St.

Guerney St.

Roxbury Crossing

Orange Line

N

3. Stuart makes his now-famous 911 call on his cellular car phone.

1. Stuart claims the assailant entered his car at this point.

2. Here is the point where Stuart claimed he and his wife were shot, and the assailant ran from the car. An injured Stuart drives off in an attempt to seek help.

Chuck's version of the events of October 23rd, 1989.
(*Map by Ellen Epstein, based on a map by Bob Monahan*/The Patriot Ledger)

Willie Bennett, the man Stuart picked out of a police line-up and identified as the assailant.
(*WCVB-TV/Picture Group*)

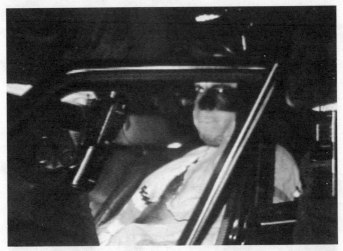

Chuck Stuart being assisted by rescue personnel in his car the night of the shootings. *(WCVB-TV/Picture Group)*

The intersection near Mission Hill where Chuck and Carol were found by rescuers and police on October 23rd. *(Ken Englade)*

Pallbearers carry the body of Carol Stuart from St. James Church in Medford after funeral services. Matthew Stuart is at the extreme left. *(AP/Wide World Photos)*

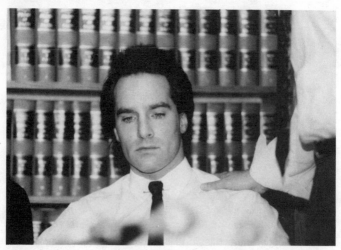

Michael Stuart during the family's news conference on January 11th, 1990. *(AP/Wide World Photos)*

Kakas & Sons, furrier at 93 Newbury Street, where Chuck worked. *(Rob Crandall/Picture Group)*

Deborah Allen, left, with her attorneys. *(Rob Crandall/Picture Group)*

The Tobin Bridge, from which Chuck Stuart allegedly jumped to his death on January 4th, 1990. *(Ken Englade)*

Following Chuck Stuart's death and Matthew Stuart's revelations, a police diver jumps from a Boston Metropolitan Police boat into the Pine River as the search for the gun used in the October shootings continues. *(AP/Wide World Photos)*

Stuart family attorney Richard Clayman, flanked by his clients *(left to right)* Shelly Yandoli, Michael Stuart, Neysa Porter and Mark Stuart, explains to the press that none of them were aware of Chuck's involvement until after the incident. *(AP/Wide World Photos)*

The Carol DiMaiti Stuart Foundation, Inc.

C/o Shawmut Bank, NA
P.O. Box 11029
Boston, MA 02211

In a gesture of healing, Evelyn and Giusto DiMaiti announce a scholarship fund in their daughter's name for youths of the Mission Hill district. *(Jim Bourg/ The New York Times)*

Carol Stuart and her baby were buried together in the DiMaiti family plot. *(Rob Crandall/Picture Group)*

An open grave awaits the coffin containing Chuck Stuart's body. *(Rob Crandall/Picture Group)*

(which for all practical purposes is synonymous with the older, less acceptable term *psychopath*), Levin strongly implied that he was one. Others, in later days, would not be so delicate. They would speak openly of "that sociopath who killed his wife and himself," with no way to prove any of the three statements. Presumably basing his comments about Chuck on what he had learned through the media, Levin launched into an explanation to keep the *Herald*'s reading public happy. "Sociopaths," he said, "don't have the capacity for remorse, for empathy. They're very manipulative, very concerned about how they present themselves. They may engage in shady business practices, or tell lies, but they don't stand out in the crowd. If they feel abandoned, that their spouse has let them down in a very profound way, they may feel it's fine to get revenge or get out of a bad situation by killing."

What Levin said, or was quoted as saying, was absolutely correct, but it was correct only as far as it went. A determination of sociopathy should be made only after a qualified examiner has had a chance to study the subject, either in person or through the reports of qualified observers. Newspaper reports of the October shooting could hardly be classified as documents upon which to base a psychological diagnosis.

The symptoms of sociopathy, which is classified as an antisocial personality disorder rather than what forensic psychiatrists and psychologists like to call "a disease of the mind," are laid out in easily understandable language in the mental health worker's bible, the *Diagnostic and Statistical Manual*, Third Edition, more commonly referred to as the *DSM III*. According to the manual, the signs of sociopathy almost always begin before the age of fifteen and usually include lying, stealing, fighting, truancy, and resisting authority. So far as is known, Chuck exhibited none of these signs. In adolescence a person suffering from this disorder also exhibits early and aggressive sexual behavior, drinks to excess, and commonly uses drugs. Again, there is no evidence that has been made public that Chuck did these things. As an adult a sociopath usually has trouble on the job, is unable to hold a job for very long, and is unable to conform to social norms. Chuck had a long history of steady, responsible employment at Kakas & Sons.

"Despite the stereotype of a normal mental status in this disorder," *DSM III* explains, "frequently there are signs of personal distress, including complaints of tension, inability to tolerate boredom, depression, and the conviction that others are hostile toward them." It continues: "Almost invariably there is markedly impaired capacity to sustain lasting, close, warm, and responsible relationships with family, friends, or sexual partners." It is possible, the manual concedes, that some sociopaths are able to achieve political and economic success, "but these people virtually never present the full picture of the disorder, lacking in particular the early onset in childhood that usually interferes with educational achievement and prohibits most public careers." True enough, Chuck's education was minimal, but it appears *not* to have been because he was suffering from mental or social problems. If he did not pursue his education as avidly as others, it seems to be because he had no interest. None of his five siblings, as far as is known, graduated from college either.

As predisposing factors toward this personality disorder, *DSM III* lists an absence of parental discipline, extreme poverty, removal from the home, and growing up without parental figures. This apparently does not apply to Chuck.

Finally, in a checklist to aid mental health workers in their diagnoses, *DSM III* lists nine major manifestations for sociopathy and recommends that four of them be present before diagnosing the disorder: "1. Inability to sustain consistent work behavior . . . ; 2. Lack of ability to function as a responsible parent . . . ; 3. Failure to accept social norms with respect to lawful behavior [as examples it lists repeated thefts, engaging in illegal occupations such as pimping, fencing, selling drugs] . . . ; 4. Inability to maintain enduring attachment to a sexual partner as indicated by two or more divorces . . . desertion of spouse, promiscuity [which it defines as having ten or more sexual partners within a year]; 5. Irritability and aggressiveness, as indicated by repeated physical fights or assaults . . . including spouse or child beating; 6. Failure to honor financial obligations . . . ; 7. Failure to plan ahead; 8. Disregard for the truth as indicated by repeated lying . . . ; and 9. Recklessness, as indicated by driving while intoxicated or recurrent speeding."

Ten days later the *Globe* published its first psychological profile. It did not imply as strongly as the *Herald* had done that Chuck was a sociopath, but it went to considerable lengths to explain what a personality disorder was and how it could be recognized. The reporter on the story, Alison Bass, seemed instead to be referring to Chuck as a narcissist, which is a first cousin to a sociopath. Or, as summarized by Dr. Charles Ford, one of the *Globe* sources and a psychiatrist at the University of Arkansas for Medical Sciences, "Sociopaths are narcissistic people without any conscience."

A narcissist, according to the *DSM III*, suffers from, among other things, "a grandiose sense of self-importance or uniqueness." A narcissist may tend to realistically overestimate his or her abilities and achievements and may submit to fantasies in which he or she achieves unlimited wealth, power, brilliance, or ideal love. "Individuals with this disorder are constantly seeking admiration and attention, and are more concerned with appearances than with substance," the manual says. According to the *DSM III*, narcissists may also suffer from the antisocial personality disorder—that is, they may be sociopathic as well. That is what the *Globe* apparently was getting at when its story segued from narcissists to sociopaths.

As with sociopathy, the *DSM III* lists criteria for diagnosing narcissists. It lists five major manifestations, three besides the exaggerated sense of self-importance and the tendency to fantisize about success. Other things to watch for are exhibitionism, cool indifference or marked feelings of rage, and two of four characteristics it lists for interpersonal relationships. These four are an expectation of special favors from others, taking advantage of others for their own desires, relationships that fluctuate between idealization and devaluation of others, and a lack of empathy.

It was, perhaps, only coincidence when the *Globe*'s Sally Jacobs wrote a long profile of Chuck almost two weeks after Bass's article on narcissism, in which she highlighted the very factors that the Bass story listed as symptoms of narcissism. After opening her piece with a tale about how Chuck was so vain that he had his hairdresser touch up his few gray hairs, she stressed that he wore expensive suits and an expensive watch, that he belonged to a health club and kept a bicycle exercise machine in his basement, that he lied about having a football scholarship to Brown, and that after his surgery he asked his friends to run errands for him—all evidence of his manipulative ability and narcissistic traits. She didn't mention his concern about his colostomy bag.

But the Bass story on narcissism was only one in the *Globe* that touched on the psychological angles of the case. The day after Bass's story, Christina Robb wrote a long, heavy piece about Jungian thought and how that school of psychoanalysis delved into "the shadow," with the shadow apparently being the Hyde side of Dr. Jekyll. All of this, in a way, fit with a phrase that was creeping into news reports with some regularity—the one about Chuck's "dark side."

In any event, Robb managed to tie the school of analytic thought (named after psychoanalyst Carl Gustav Jung) into the Stuart case. Robb's primary source, a Jungian psychoanalyst from Medford named Penelope A. Tarasuk, said Chuck's actions fit within a Jungian interpretation. "It's always shocking," Tarasuk was quoted as saying, "when somebody [i.e., Chuck] projects their own darkness onto somebody like William Bennett."

The next paragraph, which was not in quotation marks and therefore presumably reflects the personal opinion of the author, Robb, reads:

> If Charles Stuart actually did everything his brother and the police and other investigators are saying he did, he committed many crimes. One of the worst was treason against the city. He conned us into believing that he did nothing, when he did the worst things we can imagine. He conned many of us with our most unworthy fears, the ones we scare ourselves with after we've projected our worst, most unconscious impulses onto poor black men. He made us accomplices in framing an innocent man, an innocent neighborhood.

Not to be outdone, the *Herald* rebounded with another story purporting to explain Chuck's mental health. It was headlined "ALL-AMERICAN SOCIOPATH" and had a subhead reading, "Meticulous Behavior a Telling Sign." The writer, Patricia Mangan, went back to sociologist Levin and asked him to expand upon his earlier statements. The story was printed January 14, ten days after Chuck's body was found. By then Levin had had more time to study the situation, and his thoughts were more organized. "There were so many clues," he told Mangan. "Look at the way he manipulated public opinion by using the inner-city, drug-addicted criminal. Then there was the eulogy he wrote, his talk about the baby."

Levin left no doubt that he still felt that Chuck

was a sociopath and that his suicide (which also appeared to be a given to Levin) was motivated not by remorse, but by regret because he realized he had not committed the perfect murder. Levin added: "A sociopath lacks the capacity for remorse, but not for regret."

To drive its point home still one more time, the *Herald* printed another story in which Chuck was painted not only as a sociopath, but as a wife abuser as well.

In an article headlined PREGNANT AND BATTERED, STUART SHOCKER IS A CLASSIC DOMESTIC-VIOLENCE PROFILE, reporter Jim Hight delved into a different perspective of Chuck's life. What he found, he wrote, was that Chuck had "left a haunting question for everyone who had once mourned his loss: How could any man kill the mother of his unborn child?"

His finding:

> An answer comes from people who say they've seen the likes of Charles Stuart before. . . . Professionals who work with battered women, and those who counsel battering men, say the portrait of Charles Stuart that has emerged after his death matches a common profile for a perpetrator of domestic violence: a professional man with a seamless public image, driven by his business goals and secretly resentful of his family duties.
>
> And experts say Carol Stuart was in a position that exposes women to high levels of danger for abuse: she was pregnant.

Chuck could have been considered a professional. He had a seamless public image. He may or may not have been driven by his business goals. And if he was resentful of his family duties, it was very secretive. However, one thing was certain: Carol *was* pregnant. But these things in themselves do not make Chuck a wife abuser.

A wife abuse specialist quoted in *The New York Times* said it was extremely unusual for a man to begin abusing his wife by killing her. Usually, said Dr. Richard J. Gelles, a sociologist and dean of the College of Arts and Sciences at the University of Rhode Island, violence against a spouse is an escalating process. "I'd say we've interviewed ten thousand people in the last twenty years, and that includes a reasonable number of people who used guns and knives on each other. But I have never talked to anyone or met anyone who, when they decided to be violent, did it the first time by picking up a knife or a gun. There was always a slap or a shove first."

These allegations may one day prove to be true: that Chuck was a narcissist, a sociopath, a wife abuser, a murderer, a suicide. But if they are in fact proven, the proof did not come from the scant amount of evidence that was available when those stories were written. But the fact that they *were* written shows the feeling of desperation that must have been seeping into Boston city rooms, an apparent attempt to assuage the feeling of guilt for not having earlier been more skeptical and for not allowing that skepticism to be known. To imply that Chuck was a narcissist and a potential murderer because he had his hair touched up and wore expensive suits is as meaningless as the news report that said when police searched Chuck's home they found a copy of Joe McGinniss's book, *Blind Faith*.

The reporter went on to explain that the plot involved a man who had had his wife killed for insurance money, implying that Chuck may have used the book as an instruction manual to help him get rid of Carol.

By writing that Chuck was a sociopath, and that sociopaths can blend so successfully into the population that even professionals have trouble detecting them, the media were attempting to excuse themselves for not having uncovered his elaborate lie to begin with.

The knowledge that they missed the *real* story from the beginning may have prompted the editors to go as overboard as they did. Aside from that, the mentally disturbed label may have been attached early to Chuck, perhaps undeservedly, for a good reason: it made it easier for the public in general to believe a man could do what he was accused of doing only because he was severely unbalanced. In reality that is not always the case. As one Boston psychologist put it, not every man who kills his wife and then lies in an attempt to cover it up is a sociopath.

In Chuck's case, such a diagnosis is certainly open to question, subject, as are so many other issues, to the disclosure of more information, information that has not been forthcoming from authorities.

Chapter 15

By the weekend the Boston media were beginning to focus tightly on what Chuck's motive may
have been. The consensus was money. Jack Harper,
a reporter from WCVB-TV, had gone on the air the
day Chuck's body was recovered, saying that Chuck
had taken out $600,000 in life insurance on his
wife. He could not substantiate his report. When
the *Globe* hit the newsstands and front porches at
dawn, its readers also were told the motive was
insurance money. Although the headline promised
revelations about Chuck's alleged greed, the story
was thin on details. That is because there were
none. Kevin Cullen, whose byline was on the main
story, confessed in the ninth paragraph that investigators were "frustrated" in attempts to pin down

just how many policies were outstanding and what the amounts were. Initially an unidentified source said the policies totaled half a million dollars. Later that figure would be doubled. But if the police had such evidence, they didn't share it with the media. At that stage the only policy investigators were talking about was one for $82,000, which was a group policy that Carol had taken out through her employer. Not surprisingly, Chuck was the beneficiary.

The *Herald* scored a coup by reporting that Matthew had a companion with him on October 23, when he discarded Carol Stuart's jewelry, but then it shot itself in the foot with other stories that flew off on several tangents at once. It claimed that an unidentified witness had come forward who said Chuck had confessed to him that he'd killed his wife for the insurance money so he could pay off his gambling debts. That theory died there. And then the newspaper, in one of the apparent major reporting errors that appeared during coverage of the case, said Chuck underwent cocaine detoxification treatment at Boston City Hospital when he was admitted there after the shooting. The hospital later flatly denied the accusation, and the newspaper, while stubbornly sticking by its report, was not able to back it up. It also leveled a series of unsubstantiated charges against Chuck, saying he had a plan to rob his employer and that he had staged previous insurance scams.

In the fight to be competitive, the two newspapers were rushing into print with allegations that either would later be proved to be incorrect or could be neither proved nor disproved. Although the *Globe* had been fairly conservative up until then, it too would make its wild swings and take its share of the lumps.

By now the Chuck Stuart story totally dominated the local news, getting incredible play not only in the newspapers, but on local TV and radio stations as well. But since newspapers have more space than broadcasters have time, the sheer volume of the coverage was intimidating. To help readers find the latest developments in the case, newspapers took to grouping them on designated pages or in sections, each of which was flagged with a tagline so the reader could find the news quickly. The *Herald* initially grouped its stories under the banner STUART MURDER with subheads like "The Case," "Reaction," "Chronology," and "Commentary." Later it used a broader heading, THE STUART MUR-DERS, to group related stories. The *Globe* corraled its case-related stories under the encompassing headline THE STUART MURDER CASE. The most imaginative was the *Patriot Ledger* in suburban Quincy, which used the tagline "The Sordid Stuart Saga."

One of the big questions still remaining at that point (and even now) is what the autopsy on Chuck's body revealed. The *Globe*, as was by then standard practice in the case, quoted "a source familiar with the autopsy" as saying that the post-mortem examination revealed no traces of narcotics, which in itself contradicted the *Herald* contention that Chuck had been a cocaine addict. The source apparently did not comment about alcohol. Having to rely on an unidentified source to reveal details from an autopsy report on an alleged suicide victim, especially when the victim was the main suspect in a sensational murder case, was an extremely unsatisfactory way of reporting the news and may have been as frustrating to *Globe* editors as it was to the public. But in this instance the *Globe* apparently had no choice. The newspaper had fought *that* legal battle a few months before. And it lost.

Late in 1988 the *Globe* went into the Massachusetts Supreme Judicial Court seeking an order forcing the chief medical examiner to release three autopsy reports. The reports covered patients who had died at a state hospital in 1987, all of whom were autopsied by the medical examiner. In a series of stories about the deaths, the *Globe* said that two of the patients had committed suicide and the body of the third contained large amounts of pain-relieving drugs. The newspaper apparently wanted the autopsy reports as confirmation.

The judge agreed with the newspaper that the reports should be public record. He ordered the medical examiner to turn them over, which he did. However, the medical examiner also filed a brief saying he disagreed with the court's ruling and in the future would not turn over any other reports. Details about an autopsy, he argued, were to be treated as part of a person's medical record and were therefore privileged information. The *Globe* went back to the judge and asked him to clarify his order. He complied, ruling explicitly that all future autopsy reports in such cases would also be treated as public record. The medical examiner appealed.

In its case to the higher court, the *Globe* argued that information contained in autopsy reports that are part of a public record, such as death certificates (which are documents with considerably less detail), should also be available to the public.

The medical examiner countered with the argument that autopsies performed by physicians are diagnostic in nature, and since they yield detailed, intimate information about that person's physical condition, they should be considered medical records and thereby confidential.

The appeals court agreed with the medical examiner, pointing out that certain medical records, such as hospital records, results of AIDS tests, records pertaining to venereal disease, and reports of infectious diseases, were already specifically exempted from the disclosure law. The legislature also had already provided for the release of some autopsy reports, specifically citing those of persons who died in jail (in which case the autopsy report would go only to the next of kin) or to a defendant charged with murder. If the legislature had wanted to give the public access to other autopsy reports, it would have done so, the court ruled. But until it did, the court said it had no alternative but to rule against the *Globe*. To decide otherwise would be "to distort the plain statutory language," and the disclosure of such reports would constitute "a clearly unwarranted invasion of personal privacy."

Apparently none of the news organizations in town felt it was worth another court fight to try to get access to Chuck's and Carol's autopsy reports. This was unfortunate because the reports likely contain valuable information, particularly about the gunshot wounds and their angles of entry. If it can be substantiated that Carol was almost certainly shot from the backseat, as some investigators have hinted may be the case, then it could be deduced that Chuck either had to climb into the rear of the car to shoot her or a third person was involved. Similarly, if it could be determined that Chuck's wound was not self-inflicted, or if there was physical evidence to indicate he may not have voluntarily leaped off the Tobin Bridge, that could open a whole new field of inquiry.

According to the *Globe*, investigators also were beginning to question Matthew's account of what happened the night Carol and Chuck were shot. But if they were turning up any incriminating information, they kept it to themselves. The *Globe* story, woven mainly from interviews with Matthew's friends and family members, quoted an unidentified cousin as saying that Matthew was extremely loyal to Chuck since he thought his oldest brother was "virtually God."

Another cousin, also unidentified, conceded that Matthew knew Chuck was involved in some sort of illegal activity but probably did not think it was going to be a shooting. "He knew his brother was in some sort of scheme," the cousin told the *Globe*, "but to go from insurance fraud to this type of tragedy is a horrific leap. Matthew is a twenty-three-year-old man, but there are some things you never get over, and tagging along with your older brother may be one of them."

One relative who was willing to speak on the record, a rarity, was Patrick Reardon, owner of the bar where Shelly worked and where her brothers liked to hang out. He reckoned that Matthew went along because Chuck asked him to, although he had no idea what he was really getting into. "It was a big brother telling a little brother a good way to make a buck," Reardon said. "Anybody else in their right mind would have said, 'Chuckie, you're crazy.'"

Among the family, at least from what the cousins told the *Globe*, there was little doubt that Matthew was telling anything but the truth, that he had been a naive youth misled by an older brother whom he idolized.

It was October 24 all over again, with Matthew's name substituted for Chuck's and Chuck assuming the role of the black assailant. Seemingly no one could be found who wanted to say anything detrimental about Matthew or make any comment that would not excuse his action. Except one. The *Globe* uncovered a single source who hinted that Matthew might not be as conscientious as he had been painted thus far. The interviewee, referred to as "a family friend who did not want to be named," said he felt Matthew did not go to authorities to save Willie Bennett. "Matthew's no knight in shining armor," the man said. "He did it to save himself." The man apparently was referring to what he interpreted as an attempt by Matthew to go to authorities before they came to him, thus insuring possible immunity from prosecution. How successful Matthew would be would not be determined until much, much later.

10:30 A.M.

While the newspapers fought it out in black and white and the TV stations dueled with color footage, Chuck Stuart was quietly memorialized in a subdued, secretive service in the 102-year-old wooden church in which he had once served as an altar boy.

A reporter who had been stationed at the Immaculate Conception Church in Revere in anticipation of the service approached a husky, official-looking man when people began filing into the building.

"Is this the Charles Stuart funeral?" he asked.

"No," the man snapped. "This is the Pazzola funeral. Stuart won't be buried until Monday."

Reporters knew better. An hour before, two men who were known to be friends of Chuck's had shown up wearing what apparently was ubiquitous clothing in Boston: jogging suits. They went inside the funeral home, stayed a few minutes, then came out and circled the block several times. Then they went into a health spa across the street from the church and took positions at a window opening onto the street. They did not try to go inside the church and left when the service was over.

Confirmation that the funeral was Chuck's came when Charles Sr. arrived, looking aged and creaky, wearing a short tan coat over a neat dark suit. He and Chuck's mother, Dorothy, red-eyed and weary, sat in a front pew of the church that was still decorated with Christmas poinsettias. Nearby was Chuck's bronze-colored casket, covered with roses.

Unlike Carol's funeral, which had been attended by more than eight hundred people, including the governor, the police chief, the mayor, and the city's highest-ranking Roman Catholic prelate, Chuck's service was attended by fewer than one hundred mourners, discounting reporters. No one from Carol's family attended.

Brian Parsons, who had read Chuck's message at Carol's funeral, was silent at his friend's. The eulogy was delivered by the Reverend Richard Messina, who had never met Chuck. "We cannot explain the events of the past," he said, adding prophetically, "And we may never understand them."

As Chuck's siblings looked grim and his parents wept, Messina continued. "I believe all of us come from God and that all of us will eventually go to God, even though we may indulge in the ways of the sinful and, yes, violent world. But even in our last moments, I believe God reaches out and touches our hearts; that he calls out to us. I believe that in the afterlife we are given the opportunity to make amends for our sins. For some it may take longer than others, but in the end we all return to God."

When the priest distributed communion, among those going forward to receive the sacrament was Matthew, who was dressed in a dark suit and striped shirt, his curly hair tumbling below his collar. Matthew wept several times during the service and was comforted by an unidentified young woman.

After the mass, Matthew helped his father into a waiting limousine. Although he had been a pallbearer at his sister-in-law's funeral, he did not help carry Chuck's casket. That task was performed, sadly, by funeral home employees.

Although Chuck's casket was taken to nearby Woodlawn Cemetery, it was not immediately lowered into the ground. Workers said it would be buried later at an undisclosed location. Family members apparently feared that feeling against Chuck was running so high in Boston that attempts might be made to desecrate his grave.

From the cemetery, the family went to Patrick Reardon's bar, where a buffet had been set up in a back room. Conversation was muted, all but drowned out at times by shouts from the front of the tavern, where the football playoffs were being shown on a large television.

Chapter 16

January 7, 1990

With the turbulence of an unexpected winter storm, Debbie Allen blew into public consciousness on January's first Sunday via the front page of the *Globe*. It was a bright, glorious day, but the sun probably offered little cheer to Chuck's former co-worker. Although she was not initially identified by name, a headline occupying all but one of the newspaper's columns shrieked, PROBERS LINK STUART, WOMAN, and then, in a subhead, added, "Possible Romance Seen as One Motive."

Running adjacent to a grim picture of an obviously infirm Charles Stuart, Sr., being supported on one side by a grimacing Matthew and on the other by daughter Neysa Porter, the story said that the woman (who would soon be identified as Debbie Allen) visited Chuck at the hospital and, using his telephone credit card, called him frequently while he was receiving treatment. It also said Chuck had bought a 14-karat-gold brooch to give to her for her birthday, which was the day before he died.

The *Globe* story noted that the woman refused to talk to reporters when they tried to intercept her as she was leaving a meeting with investigators, but the newspaper quoted police sources as saying it was the second time she had been interviewed by investigators. The first session had taken place in late October.

Twenty-four hours later the *Globe* had a second piece in which she was not only identified, but her picture was published. Grainy and shadow-splotched, the picture showed a blonde, her hair falling below her shoulders, maneuvering around a parked car. The cutline said it was a picture of Allen outside her home in suburban Millis.

An avid figure skater and ice hockey player, Allen had graduated from Brown University in the spring of 1989 and enrolled the following autumn in the MBA program at Babson College. She lived at home with her parents and two brothers.

Three days later, apparently feeling the heat and the need to comment, Allen issued a statement through a lawyer, Thomas Dwyer. She and Chuck had been friends since she started as a summer employee at Kakas & Sons two years before, she said, but the relationship had never been a physical one.

"I was never romantically involved with Charles Stuart," she said in her statement. "I socialized with him both alone and with others on a few occasions. On more than one occasion, both Stuarts described their marriage to me in warm and loving terms."

After the shooting, she said, she called Chuck to express her sympathy. He asked her to visit him in the hospital, but she demurred at first on grounds that she did not think it appropriate. However, she relented when he told her that others from Kakas & Sons had been stopping by. One time, she said, and one time only, she and her boyfriend, along with a female friend of hers, went to BCH.

After that, Chuck asked her to call him, but she put him off, saying the calls would show up on her family telephone bill and her parents would not approve. At that point Chuck gave her his telephone credit card and told her to use it instead. She did not say how often or how many times she telephoned him, but police said there were "numerous" calls, both to the hospital and to Chuck's parents' house after he was released.

"In our conversations," the statement said stiffly, "Mr. Stuart told me about his physical condition and his visitors. I tried to distract him by telling him about graduate school and my friends."

By late December Allen was beginning to worry about the continuing relationship, and she turned for advice to her boyfriend and the female friend who had gone with her on the hospital visit. They concluded that she should break off the relationship, that Chuck "no longer needed her constant support" and it was time for him "to grieve on his own." She called to tell him that, she said, and that was her last conversation with him.

After the shooting, she said she had no reason to doubt Chuck's story about being shot by a black gunman, nor did she doubt him when he told her that he had recognized the assailant during the lineup. He never hinted to her that he might have shot his wife. In her statement she did not refer to published reports quoting two of her friends as saying that Chuck had asked her soon after the shooting not to contradict what he had told police about the incident.

And the only presents Chuck had ever given her, she said, were "a pair of sneakers, a sweatshirt, and a joke gift." For her twenty-third birthday on January 3 he had sent her a card. He did *not* give her a brooch or any other jewelry, she insisted.

After reading Allen's statement, Dwyer told reporters that he had no doubt that Chuck wanted to extend the relationship beyond friendship. "But there is also no question that prior to his death, Debbie Allen made it quite clear to Mr. Stuart that the minimal relationship they had was over." Then he added mysteriously: "Police possess a document wherein Mr. Stuart himself characterizes his relationship with Ms. Allen as one based solely on friendship."

Police, not surprisingly, refused to comment on the enigmatic "document" or say why they thought the relationship had been more serious than Allen was willing to admit.

Clearly, Allen and Dwyer intended her statement to be the last word on the subject. Whether that, indeed, will be the case remains to be seen. Conceivably Allen could be called before the grand jury or any other group with subpoena power that is charged with looking into the matter.

To rebut the *Herald*'s earlier report that Chuck

had undergone treatment for drug withdrawal as well as for his gunshot wound, Boston City Hospital's chief of surgery, Dr. Erwin Hirsch, granted an interview to the *Globe*. Although he still left a lot of questions unanswered, Hirsch revealed previously undisclosed details about Chuck's stay. He was suffering from "a very, very serious wound," the physician said. "He was a sick cookie." Hirsch's apparent goal in agreeing to the interview was to shoot down news reports that said Chuck underwent treatment for drug addiction at the same time he was being treated for his gunshot wound. The physician jumped to that subject right away. "His care had nothing to do with drugs," Hirsch stressed, adding, however, that someone not familiar with the case may have gotten that impression because Chuck was a participant in a new pain-control program. He did not elaborate about the program or say someone may have confused it with drug detoxification.

Did he think Chuck shot himself?

The doctor thought about that, then answered slowly, "I've heard all the rumors, but when you ask me, 'Did I suspect at any time that his wounds were self-inflicted?' the answer is no."

This was an intriguing comment. If the chief of surgery at the hospital Chuck was taken to immediately after he was found wounded in his car, the hospital where he was given emergency treatment, the hospital where he underwent two operations, and the hospital where he was kept for six weeks, if neither Hirsch nor his staff, who knew Chuck's medical condition better than anyone before or since, never suspected that the wound was self-inflicted, then either Chuck did such a good job of turning the gun on himself that it did not attract even professional attention, or the wound was not self-inflicted. If the former is true, he was either very lucky or very skilled, more likely lucky. If the wound was not self-inflicted, then a third party was involved, and that would open up a whole new array of possibilities. Disappointingly, Hirsch was not asked to speculate on that angle. But he probably would not have answered in any case. What it means for the public, though, is that the question will never be answered, unless one of three things occurs: 1. Investigators or prosecutors suddenly become very forthcoming; 2. A grand jury investigates the issue and releases a report; 3. Someone confesses. At this stage, none of these options appears likely.

Asked if he could squelch the report that Allen visited Chuck while he was recuperating, Hirsch said there "absolutely was not" a woman fitting that description who ever visited him. The only women he remembers coming to see him were his mother and his two half sisters. Other visitors included brothers Michael and Mark, the DiMaitis, and a number of cousins. "The only one I don't remember being there was Matthew," said Hirsch, which made sense because Matthew had gone to California soon after the shooting and did not return until Chuck had been released. Hirsch later would be contradicted about Allen's presence at the hospital by her best friend, who said she, Allen, and Allen's boyfriend visited Chuck at least once.

* * *

Anxious not to be accused of doing a sloppy job of beating the bushes this time around, the *Globe* and the *Herald* went all out to give as broad a picture as possible of developments in the case. Despite their individual attempts to organize the disparate articles, readers still got the impression that they were having bits of information fired at them from a shotgun. However, pellets of fact that were scattered from one end of the respective publications to the other and had to be meticulously gathered, turned up a number of interesting items.

The *Globe*:

- Reported that police had discovered Chuck's safe in its basement hideaway and when they got inside it found a $100,000 insurance policy on his wife. This was in addition to the $82,000 policy Carol had at work.

- Said investigators were trying to track down a man who had told several people that Chuck had asked him to kill his wife. This allegedly happened weeks before the October shooting. But when a homicide detective went to the man before Christmas and asked him to repeat his story, the man refused. There was nothing the police could do.

- Published an article by its star columnist, Mike Barnicle, brother of a detective, that heaped dubious praise upon the Boston police. "When this incredibly bizarre story finally comes to an end," he wrote, "it will be shown that detectives from the homicide unit merely covered themselves with glory." They earned such acclamation, Barnicle said, because they charged Willie Bennett only with armed robbery and not the murder of

Carol and Christopher. "Perhaps reluctance
came because they knew him and understood
that Bennett did not finish the seventh grade."
His IQ, Barnicle said, was 62, and he was classified by the school system as a "mental defective."
Barnicle questioned how anyone, knowing Bennett's history, could champion his cause or, even
more puzzling, use it as an example of bigotry in
Boston. "Willie Bennett is a sociopath," the columnist contended, not noting the irony in which
his newspaper and its rival were jockeying to see
who could get the most authoritative expert to
say that Chuck was the sociopath in the case.

- Devoted the single remaining column at the top
of page one to a heartrending story by Eileen
McNamara telling about the "other suicide" on
the Tobin Bridge. Just thirty-two hours before
Stuart allegedly leaped to his death from the
bridge, twenty-year-old Paul Horne jumped from
the same structure. But his death went unher-
alded, and no one seemed to care except his
family and a friend who had taken the time to
call the newspaper. Unlike the ambiguity surrounding Chuck, there was little doubt that
Horne was a suicide. Earlier on the day of his
death, the twenty-year-old Horne contacted a
friend, George Lyons, a counselor who helped
him in high school, and told him he was going to
kill himself. Lyons tried to convince him to return to the psychiatric clinic in Brookline where
he had been receiving treatment. He even lent
Horne train fare for the trip. Instead of returning
to the hospital, Horne hailed a taxi in front of a
Revere supermarket at 10:31 P.M. Tuesday and
asked to be taken into Boston. When the taxi
stopped at the toll booth on the bridge, Horne
threw open the door, jumped out of the cab, and,

without hesitating, vaulted over the rail. Horne's body was one of those that never made it to the river. He had leaped from the upper deck rather than the lower one, as Chuck allegedly had done, and his body smashed into the roadway on the lower level. As a final irony, when Horne's aunt called from Florida to verify the death, she was told the victim couldn't have been her nephew because the bridge jumper had been Chuck Stuart.

There were, however, several major differences between Horne's death and Chuck's. Horne had a history of mental problems and was currently under treatment. He had tried twice before, unsuccessfully, to kill himself. He was known to be deeply depressed. He told a friend what he was going to do. And he had a witness to his act.

The *Herald*:
- Since it did not yet have the Debbie Allen angle, its main story focused on the fact that Matthew had not been alone at the Dizzy Bridge that night and that investigators appeared to be suspicious of Matthew's story.
- It did not go as heavy on the "other woman" angle as the *Globe* had done, but it said that *two* women were being questioned to see if they were romantically involved with Chuck. Since the *Herald* had also doubled the amount of alleged insurance to $1 million, it was enough to make one wonder if there was not a campaign in the *Herald* newsroom simply to multiply the *Globe's* accusations by a factor of two.
- Reluctant to give up on its cocaine angle, the *Herald* also quoted unnamed prosecutors as acknowledging that they knew that Chuck had the

drug in his system on the night of October 23. Since Hirsch's denial, however, and the fact that the medical records apparently were going to be locked away forever, it looked as though the tabloid were fighting a war it could not win.

- It touched on an item that even it considered too far out to approach on its own. Buried deep in its main story were a couple of paragraphs quoting the *Daily Evening Item* in suburban Lynn as saying that a security camera at Brigham and Women's had recorded a sequence showing Chuck beating Carol in the hospital parking lot on the night of the shooting. Prosecutors and police denied it, as did the firm contracted to provide security for the hospital.

- The *Globe* had its mystery man who said Chuck had approached him about a way to kill his wife, so the *Herald* found one as well. Sort of. Near the bottom of its main story, the newspaper, timidly for a publication that had already convicted Chuck of murder with terms like "his monstrous murder-for-money scheme," said that six months before the shooting Chuck had approached "another family member" and asked him if he knew how he could go about hiring someone to kill Carol. It attributed the report to another unnamed family member. Ironically, both the *Herald* and the *Globe* would prove to be right on that issue, but it was a development that would not break for days. And when it did it would be in bold headlines, it would not be tucked away inconspicuously deep into a round-up story.

On the political front, Mayor Flynn and Police Commissioner Roache met on Saturday, January 6, with black leaders and representatives of the Mission Hill neighborhood to try to resolve the difficulties that had surfaced since Chuck's body was found.

Flynn promised that he and Roache would go door to door in the poorer neighborhoods for "as long and as often" as necessary to try to ease concerns about the way the investigation was handled.

Apparently the mayor's peace moves were meeting with some success. One of his visits had been to Mission Church in Mission Hill, where one of those he met with was Maria Sanchez, a member of a group called Puerto Rican Tenants of Mission Hill in Action. Sanchez had been particularly critical of Flynn, saying that the U.S. invasion of Panama was a skirmish compared with the Boston PD's invasion of Mission Hill. After Flynn's visit, though, she appeared mollified, saying she considered it an apology to the neighborhood.

Most of his other critics, however, were not so easily subdued. Cries were raised anew for his and Roache's resignations, to which Flynn replied hotly that he was elected by the voters and had no intention of resigning. As far as Roache was concerned, he was Flynn's appointee and still had his confidence. "There is no question in my mind about whether or not he should stay on," he told the group, a response that failed to make anyone very happy.

Perhaps as a result of Flynn's Saturday session, a group of moderate black leaders met on Sunday, January 7, in the home of former State Representative Melvin H. King to plan a more reasoned response to the crisis that was gripping the minority communities. More than two dozen people were present. During the three-hour session, they agreed to carry their grievances up the line from City Hall. They would ask, they said, for state and federal inquiries into the conduct not only of police, but also of prosecutors and the news media. "We're not calling for anyone's resignation," said State Representative Byron Rushing. "What we're trying to do is pause for a moment and figure out what happened. Once we have all the pieces of the puzzle, then we can make some sensible decision about what should happen next."

What they would like to see happen, they said, was for the U.S. attorney to investigate the case and determine if the civil rights of Willie Bennett and Alan Swanson had been violated, plus determine the constitutionality of the stop-and-search policy. They also would like to see the creation of a commission to look at the case beyond the civil rights questions.

"What we're finding out," said Rushing, "is that reporters heard rumors, people in the community heard rumors, people in the hospital heard rumors. Why weren't these rumors investigated?" Were reporters, he asked, discouraged from investigating the incident by their editors, police, or prosecutors? Other issues involved were whether police followed the proper investigatory procedure in the case and why Bennett was placed in a lineup when he had not been charged in connection with the Stuart shooting.

"People are asking what we want," said Rushing.

"They want to know how we can prevent this from happening again. I don't think we can make any informed judgments about that until we know what happened."

It was certainly a more restrained approach than any proposed so far. However, that group did not represent the more militant faction of the black community, which was still screaming for Flynn's head. Even while the group of moderates was meeting in one section of the city, Flynn and Roache were huddled with still another, angrier, group that demanded two things from the mayor: first, that he issue a formal apology to the minority community for the way the case had been handled; and second, that he create a citizen's review board with oversight power over the police department.

Flynn left the session two hours later without responding officially to either demand. "I've said on a number of occasions that I regret the way the case was handled," he told reporters, "and I would like to see somebody apologize to the entire city of Boston." He admitted, however, that he was cold to the review board proposal.

Chapter 17

From the time the Stuart case took its dramatic turn with Chuck's death and Matthew's story to the District Attorney, the Boston media, particularly the newspapers, tried to balance news stories with analysis, interpretation, and comment. Sometimes they were successful; sometimes they were not. The *Herald* seemed particularly prone to folding editorial material into its news reports. And the analysis that was presented was not always enlightening or pertinent; witness the blatant determination to label Chuck a sociopath when such a conclusion should be a critical psychological finding based upon more solid evidence than had been presented thus far. Sometimes, too, it was difficult for all but the careful reader to tell what was analysis and what was news, particularly since neither paper made an attempt to differentiate with readily visible labels. The front page of the *Globe* on January 9 was a prime example. Under a single headline

streaming across the top of page one—PROBERS SAY
DISCLOSURES WOULD HAVE MADE DIFFERENCE—were
two stories, one news and one, presumably, analysis.

The news story, in the top right hand spot, carried the subhead "Gun Not Reported Missing Until
After Suicide" and was a wrap-up detailing most
of the appropriate events of the past twenty-four
hours, highlighting the fact that Jay Kakas did not
report the company's pistol missing until after
Chuck's death.

The other story, by staffer Peter J. Howe, carried
the subhead "Many Kept Clues about Stuart to
Themselves." Although it was a faithful chronicle
of a growing list of people who knew or had good
reason to suspect that Chuck was more deeply
involved in his wife's shooting than had been revealed before Matthew went to the investigators, it
also weaved in enough comment to prevent it from
being classified as news. But there was no attempt
by *Globe* editors to signal this distinction. While
the story made some interesting points, some of
them were open to argument. At one point, Howe
wrote:

> After Stuart's suicide, two neighbors in Reading
> told reporters about loud fights they remember the
> couple having or said Carol Stuart complained
> repeatedly that her husband went out alone on
> Friday nights and stayed out late.

Disregarding the assertion, the assumed given,
that Chuck's death was a suicide, the text strongly
implies that 1) this behavior was a valuable clue

to Chuck's murderous intent, and 2) if police had possessed this information the previous autumn, it might have pointed them toward Chuck immediately and the Willie Bennett episode would never have happened. Admittedly this information shows that Chuck and Carol did not have the perfect marriage, but the "perfect marriage" was an illusion carefully created by the media, including the *Globe*, to begin with. The fact that the marriage was imperfect is hardly surprising. What is more surprising is that no one challenged the media concept sooner. But if the marriage was not totally trouble free, that still did not indicate that Chuck was planning to kill his wife. *Every* couple argues, sometimes heatedly. It is not rare for the differences to be so great that the marriage falls apart. But hundreds of thousands of marriages a year break up without either spouse resorting to murder. Besides that, the fact that they argued occasionally and that Carol might not have liked her husband spending Friday nights with the guys showed that they were human, that their marriage probably was like every other marriage, with its ups and downs, celebrations and conflicts. What investigators may well have concluded from this information about family fights is that despite occasional tiffs the Stuarts still had a solid marriage.

Howe again:

Some friends knew that Charles Stuart had a strong interest for several months before the shooting in a Millis woman, then 21 years old, who had worked for two summers at the fur store where Stuart was a manager. Police sources said they had a romantic relationship that began in July, and they said they believe the woman, Deborah J. Allen, was the intended recipient of a $250 gold brooch he bought the day before her birthday last week.

The implication here is that Chuck and Allen were romantically involved and that the police knew it, and may have known it since the first time they questioned Allen in October. Although that may one day prove to be the case, it was not known with certainty at the time. And even if it were, that in itself did not constitute a surefire motive for murder. Neither did the possibility that Chuck was probably attracted physically to a very comely young woman with whom he had been thrown into daily contact. All over the country, every day, businessmen develop sexual attractions for their secretaries (and vice versa), salespeople for their clients, co-workers for each other. But most of those attractions remain in the fantasy realm, and many marriages continue to hold together despite these real or imagined lapses. And even the ones that do break up generally end more peacefully than with murder.

For inflammatory comments, however, it was hard to beat the *Globe*'s Mike Barnicle. The difference between Barnicle's articles and the other apparent analysis pieces was that the former were clearly understood to be opinion. It was when Barnicle was a co-byliner on the news stories that things began to get fuzzy. Since there were virtually no named sources in the stories, and since most assertions were unsubstantiated, it was difficult to tell when his opinion was masquerading as fact, when he was using police locker room scuttlebutt camouflaged as knowledge. But when he was writing under his single byline, with his name in white capital letters inside a black box, he could say what he felt—and he felt a lot. To call him outspoken would be an understatement. On January 7 he wrote about Chuck Stuart:

> It is a measure of the depth of one man's icy, calculating, maniacal cruelty that, hours before the infant expired, Chuck Stuart asked to be wheeled alongside the child's incubator to say goodbye.

And a couple of paragraphs later:

> . . . this man, a cunning demon capable of fooling nearly everyone around him and almost all those charged with investigating his wife's murder, hurled himself off the bridge into the water below.

On January 10 Barnicle's column was in the spot that newspaper editors call the second lead—that is, in the upper left hand corner of page one. On that day Barnicle thought he had a great scoop. He had discovered, he felt, that Chuck planned Carol's murder so he could open his own restaurant. Plus, on the day that Chuck died he was due to collect on a $480,000 life insurance policy from the Prudential Insurance Company. In Barnicle's words:

> Last night . . . [a] man sat at a desk downtown and stared in amazement at a piece of paper that finally provided a motive for this crime that has damaged so many people and destroyed so many lives. The man sat in his chair and looked out the window as the lights of the distant buildings began

to shine like small stars in an evening when everyone talked only about the cruelty of this murder.

"He killed her so he could get money to open up a restaurant," the man was saying. "Turns out it's that simple and that pathetic. . . ."

On the other side of the front page, in the lead news spot, was a story that said much the same as Barnicle's column. The story carried dual bylines: Kevin Cullen and Mike Barnicle. The first two paragraphs of the news story read:

A police diver yesterday recovered the gun investigators believe Charles M. Stuart used to kill his pregnant wife so he could collect life insurance benefits that authorities now suspect were meant to finance a new career as a restauranteur.

Sources say a check made out to Stuart for $480,000—the proceeds of a life insurance policy for his wife, Carol—had already been processed by the Prudential Insurance Co. last Thursday when Stuart killed himself.

In neither case is the benefactor of this information identified. In Barnicle's column it is "a man" slumped "at a desk downtown." In the news story coauthored by Barnicle, the information is attributed to "sources." Many journalists would have trouble with this duality of Barnicle's. Ostensibly the man is paid to pronounce his opinion, not cover news. Imagine *The New York Times* running a front-page story with William Safire listed as a coauthor or Andy Rooney doing a stand-upper for the nightly news. To make matters worse, the information appears to be dead wrong. A Prudential spokesman denied that the company had a policy issued in the name of Carol Stuart. Neither had it written a check to Charles Stuart, not on the day he died or any other day.

Nevertheless, the *Globe* continued to stand by its story even in the face of the Prudential denial. Clearly either the *Globe* was extremely confident of Barnicle's sources or it did not want to admit it had made a mistake. It is possible that the Prudential spokesman was incorrect and a check had been issued. It is also possible that Prudential did not want to confess that it had written a substantial check to an apparent murderer. But that would be foolish as well as unethical. If there was a policy on Carol's life, the money would still be paid to the beneficiary. If the beneficiary was dead, the money would go to the beneficiary's estate and would show up in court records when the estate was probated. If Prudential *were* trying to cover up, which would be the least likely scenario, it would only be able to keep the secret for so long.

There was a possibility, too, that Barnicle's sources had the amount right but the company wrong. In that case, however, it would have been to the *Globe*'s (and Barnicle's) advantage to clear up the misunderstanding as soon as possible.

There is a possibility, in fact, that the whole issue of insurance was hyped beyond belief. Despite leaks from police "sources" that Chuck had large amounts of insurance on his wife, some stories said up to $1 million, there has been no corroboration. As far as is known publicly, there were only three policies on Carol's life: one for $82,000 through her employer, one for $100,000 through the Travelers Life Insurance Company, and another for $100,000 through American Express. The *Herald* reported on February 2 that it had learned there was still a third $100,000 policy on Carol, but the report was not confirmed by any other source.

Discounting the group policy and the unlikely report in the *Herald*, if Chuck had only $200,000 insurance on Carol (just slightly more than the amount needed to cover the mortgage on their home), she probably was underinsured rather than overinsured. Life insurance agents generally recommend that an individual's policies total four to five times the amount of actual earnings. Carol made $40,000 a year, but she was only thirty and relatively fresh out of law school, her career was still in its infancy. It is not unreasonable to assume that, even if she did not become a star, she would in a few years easily double or triple what she was making at the time she was killed.

Chuck was insured for an almost identical amount. Documents made public later showed that he had two $100,000 policies and a $14,000 policy with the company for which his father once worked. Apparently that was an old policy, and the two larger policies were taken out later. His father was believed to be the beneficiary on the small policy and Carol on the two larger ones. Again, as with Carol, the two larger policies would barely cover the mortgage on their home if he were to die and leave her struggling to keep up monthly house payments.

Still a mystery is a comment Carol is supposed to have made to at least one of her friends that she and Chuck were chronically "insurance poor." Without knowing more details about the kinds of policies, it is difficult to gauge what their annual cost was. However, the $100,000 policy Chuck had on Carol through American Express, for example, was most likely for term insurance, and given Carol's age, it is doubtful that the premium was more than $250 to $300 a year.

Here we have another example of how investigators and prosecutors seemingly have worked—successfully—to obscure the details. Despite investigators' claims that there is no central data bank for policies, it is inconceivable that, in this age of computers, such a registry does not exist. Assuming that such a file is a reality, it should be a simple matter for authorities to gain access and discover precisely how much insurance money is involved. If that is the case, prosecutors and police have not made the information public.

Knowing how much insurance money is involved is crucial to understanding the dynamics of the situation. Remove insurance as a possible motive and the case against Chuck as his wife's killer suffers a substantial blow. If no considerable amount of money is involved, that also damages the restaurant-as-motive theory, and the case against Chuck grows increasingly wobbly.

The fact that Chuck would want to open a restaurant should come as no surprise; at the Voke he majored in culinary arts, and his first jobs were as a cook. On weekends, when Chuck and Carol entertained, Chuck invariably was the chef. In his January 10 column, Barnicle made an issue out of the fact that investigators found a number of restaurant trade magazines in the Reading house, along with literature on how to start a business. But as a motive for murder?

The restaurant hypothesis was shaken almost as soon as Barnicle proposed it. The day after his column was published the *Globe* ran a story by Kevin Cullen and Anthony Flint in which they quoted one of Carol's former business associates as saying that Carol was well aware of Chuck's desire to have a restaurant of his own. Such a plan, in fact, was discussed by the two of them in detail when they were trying to decide what to do with the profit from the house in Medford. In the end they agreed jointly to sink the money into the Reading house and postpone the restaurant idea.

It is possible, of course, that Chuck decided not to wait any longer. But if Carol's insurance totaled only $282,000, that was only a little more than double what he made each year and only 60 percent more than their combined annual income.

Nevertheless, Barnicle claimed he knew what Chuck's motive was. In the conclusion of his January 10 column, he shared it with his readers. In his view Carol died for the most trivial of reasons:

> She died because her husband wanted to be someone important. He wanted to have his name on a restaurant, to own something, to have people truly like, admire, and remember him. He wanted people to think he was swell, and he wanted to get where he was going in a hurry. His wife's life was merely the down payment.

Maybe. Maybe not.

Chapter 18

One way of evaluating developments in the Stuart case would be to treat the incident as if it were a natural event, such as a series of earthquakes. Chuck's death really shook the Richter scale. The biggest shock to follow Dereck Jackson's and Eric Whitney's recantations of their grand jury testimony against Willie Bennett occurred when Michael and Mark Stuart, Shelly Yandoli, and Neysa Porter gathered in Richard Clayman's law library, a meeting to which the media had been invited.

It was Clayman's show, and he took full advantage of it. The forty-two-year-old lawyer who had once worked as a former assistant district attorney under Flanagan has a reputation for flamboyance, and on this day he showed why. Stripped to his shirtsleeves with the cuffs rolled back, he pranced like a rock star in concert. He bobbed his head. He shook his shoulders. He paced. He pursed his lips. He waved his arms. He rested his hand reverently

on Michael's shoulder, on his head, like a funda-
mentalist preacher bestowing a blessing. He did
semaphores with his hands. He croaked and bellowed and whispered. He did everything but play
the bagpipes and dance. Although the Stuart siblings sat around Clayman in a serious semicircle—
Shelly, Michael, Neysa, and Mark, looking diminu-
tive against the walls of books—they may as well
been cardboard cutouts. Under strict orders from
Clayman to let him do *all* the talking, they uttered
not a word. What they would have said, had Clayman let them talk, would have been icing: the
lawyer served up the cake.

Verily, he said, the rumors about some of the
family members knowing of Chuck's role prior to
his death were true. Michael, the lawyer confirmed,
had known about Chuck's involvement within seventy-two hours of the incident. He knew because
Matthew had gone to him and told him. The others
did not know until much later. Mark and Shelly
found out on January 1 and Neysa the next day,
although Clayman was strangely vague about dates
and other specifics. But the real shocker from Clayman was the announcement that Michael had gotten a preview of what was coming, an advance peek
at what was going to happen long before Matthew
came to him.

Weeks before the October 23 shooting, in late
August or very early September (his impreciseness
with dates was either coolly deliberate or unbeliev-
ably sloppy), Clayman said Chuck pulled Michael
aside and they had a "disjointed, vague conversation" in which Chuck asked Michael if he would
help him kill someone. Whether Chuck had identi-

fied that "someone" as Carol was not clear. In any case, Michael's reaction, according to his lawyer, was to brush it off as a stupid comment.

"At that time it had no significance to Michael," Clayman said. "My client's response was a definitive 'I don't know what you're talking about, but I'm not getting involved in any sort of crazy thing you're talking about.'" No more was said about the subject, Clayman said. Not then; not later. Not even after Matthew told him what he knew about Chuck's role in the October 23 shooting.

"I reviewed that conversation with him, and it doesn't have a hell of a lot of significance," Clayman said. Pausing, he added, "But in retrospect, after examining all the data, an argument can be made that it should have had, or why didn't it, or at least now I think someone could argue that it had some significance."

Clayman's statement strained credibility. The lawyer was asking the world to believe that Chuck had asked Michael if he'd help him kill his wife. Michael had brushed it off as if it had been a dumb comment like telling him that the Atlanta Braves were going to win the World Series. Seven weeks or so later, the wife is killed. Even while Chuck is recovering from surgery from his own wound, brother Matthew comes to him and says that Chuck was involved in Carol's death. And Michael never went to Chuck and said, "Hey, remember last summer when you talked to me about killing Carol?"

Clayman's understatement hardly registered among the gathered reporters, who twitched nervously, waiting for him to finish so they could bombard him with questions. Newspeople got their chance soon enough, but they got very little new useful information.

Was there a family plot to keep silent?

No, Clayman responded firmly. "The appearance that has evolved is that some type of conspiratorial scenario existed, all these family members sitting around talking about keeping something hidden. That is not true."

Did any of the brothers or sisters go to Chuck's home while Chuck was in the hospital and remove incriminating material, such as insurance policies?

No, said Clayman. "They knew nothing about insurance. If some documents were picked up, it was not the kind of pickup that was intentional, as if they went looking for insurance papers."

Did he think that any of them, especially Michael, might be legally called to task for the role he had played in the series of events?

No, Clayman said yet again. "I am comfortable after an examination of this entire scenario that there was no violation of the law. His hands are legally clean."

Legally, maybe. But he did not say anything about morally. Still, that would hardly be Clayman's job. He was being paid to promote his client's innocence, not help pave their path into a courtroom. Whether a grand jury agreed with Clayman's assessment was yet to be seen.

Apparently concerned that the original grand jury that had begun hearing evidence in the Stuart case the previous November may have been tainted by the flap over the testimony implicating Willie Bennett, District Attorney Flanagan named a new twenty-three member panel and said it would begin immediately investigating the case, starting from the very beginning. As would later become evident, he did not specify that they should be in any rush to do so.

Despite the whirlwind of controversy around Mayor Flynn and Police Commissioner Roache, Flanagan had managed to keep pretty well out of the line of fire as far as the Stuart case went. A veteran politician, a wily expert in the ways of bureaucracies, the gray-haired, jowly district attorney knew when to stand up and shout and when to sit down and shut up.

Seemingly slow in starting his career, Flanagan went to work for District Attorney Garret H. Byrne in 1962, when he was thirty-two years old. For sixteen years he worked in a back office, keeping a low profile. But in 1978, with his boss about to turn eighty, Flanagan decided to make his move.

"It's time for a crusading district attorney," he bragged in announcing his candidacy. Flanagan won that election with ease. But it was the closest he ever got to being a crusader.

Many political observers are puzzled by Flanagan's ability to inspire confidence in voters. Despite the pledges of his first campaign, he has been anything but an aggressive prosecutor, preferring to get by as he did for most of the time he worked under Byrne—by not making waves. His critics accuse him of running a patronage shop, filled with aging white men with Irish surnames. But the voters are not listening. Flanagan has handily won each of his three reelection campaigns, and in the last race he did not even have any opposition.

His strongest support seems to come from white, Catholic voters who like him because he is a regular in the Knights of Columbus halls and a frequent participant at the ubiquitous communion breakfasts. He likes to pump hands and slap backs, and he has an apparent natural inclination to laugh quietly at himself. His trademark is his necktie, which always is the most outrageous and ostentatious he can find.

Although his personal popularity has remained high, at least among whites, and his vote-drawing power is enough of a shield to scare away formidable opposition, the professional confidence of his staff has come under increasing scrutiny. Even before the Stuart case, there were serious questions about how his men were doing their job.

In Boston, before Chuck and Carol were shot, the longest continually running headline grabber in the crime sphere was a confused legal battle referred to as the Griffiths case. What happened was this:

On February 17, 1988, Detective Sherman C. Griffiths, a member of the Boston PD's drug control unit, went to an apartment house in the Dorchester section of the city to make a narcotics bust. Approaching the apartment in which he thought the suspected drug dealer was hiding, he was shot through the door. He died instantly, without seeing who had shot him. Tucked in Griffiths's pocket was a search warrant that had been obtained after another detective, Carlos Luna, swore to the judge that he had a detailed description of the suspect, which he said had been provided by an informant.

A thirty-four-year-old Jamaican immigrant, Albert Lewin, was quickly arrested and charged with killing Griffiths, even though Lewin did not fit Luna's description of the drug dealer whom Griffiths had been on his way to arrest.

In building Lewin's defense, his lawyers asked the police department to produce Luna's informant to see if they could straighten out the matter of the non–matching description. It developed that there had been no informant; he was a figment of the police department's imagination. So was the description. Information that drugs were being dealt in the apartment had come from three different people, officers later swore, none of whom apparently could describe the dealer. So Luna made up a description so they could get a search warrant. Since no one wanted to admit this to Lewin's lawyers, Luna told them that the informant was dead.

He testified later that the idea of the imaginary informant's imaginary demise was given to him by another police officer and was "reinforced" by one of Flanagan's top assistants.

Flanagan's assistant denied the charges on the stand and has twice been vindicated of encouraging Luna to lie.

Although the case has not yet been settled, it prompted Flanagan's critics to question how far the district attorney's prosecutors would go in trying to get an arrest and conviction—an issue that erupted in full force in the Willie Bennett case. Raising even more eyebrows was the fact that the same prosecutor, Thomas Mundy, was in charge of both cases.

This was still another twist that added even more complications to the Stuart case and was a good reason for Flanagan's men not to want to disclose any more information than they absolutely had to about the Stuart investigation.

Chapter 19

Although the *Globe* had been hinting for days that there was another person to whom Chuck had confided his plans, its reporters had failed to come up with anything solid. Kudos for that accomplishment went to David Ropeik at WCVB-TV, the city's ABC affiliate.

On January 10 Ropeik aired an interview with an old high school buddy of Chuck's. Although the man appeared on the air, his identification was camouflaged electronically and his name was not divulged. The man said he had gotten a call from Chuck the previous September, which was a surprise because he had not heard from him in years. Chuck said he and Carol wanted the man and his wife to have dinner together. The man said he and his wife went and had a good time. A few days later Chuck called him again and asked him to have dinner with him alone. After they had eaten and were walking back to their cars, the man said

Chuck started telling him about how he was tired of being married to Carol and how things were just going to get worse now that they were going to have a baby. "That's going to give her the upper hand in our relationship," Chuck allegedly said, "and I can't stand that." Chuck said that Carol had refused to have an abortion, so he was going to be saddled with both a wife and a child, neither of which he wanted. To make matters worse, Carol would quit her job and they would lose her income. That would mean the end of his plans to open a restaurant, Chuck whined. Then Chuck looked the man in the eye and popped the big question: Would he help him kill Carol?

The man, who was later identified when he appeared before the grand jury as David F. MacLean, a truck driver from Lowell, said he thought Chuck was joking and passed it off with a light remark. Later, after the shooting, he remembered the conversation and mentioned it to a couple of people, one of whom told a policeman friend of his. The cop notified a detective in the homicide division, who called MacLean not long after the shooting and asked about the conversation. Frightened, MacLean denied that the talk ever occurred.

Ropeik got on to MacLean, he said, because he aired a story the day after Chuck's death quoting an unnamed family member as saying that Chuck had confessed to shooting Carol. According to *that* source, Chuck said he'd done it for the insurance money. The family member said Chuck admitted shooting Carol, then turning the gun on himself. He planned to shoot himself in the foot, Chuck is alleged to have said, but his hand jerked when he pulled the trigger and he wounded himself in the stomach instead. If that indeed was the case, it was a twitch that almost proved fatal.

It was after this story was broadcast, Ropeik said, that he received a call from the man, who later turned out to be MacLean. Although MacLean refused to identify himself to the reporter at the time, Ropeik used clues he had gotten from his source on the Chuck-confession story to track him down and convince him to tell his tale on tape.

MacLean is believed to have repeated the story he told Ropeik to the new grand jury when it held its first session on January 12. Also called to testify at the opening meeting were Jay Kakas and Gary McLaughlin.

After a single day of testimony, the grand jury recessed indefinitely at the request of the Stuart case prosecutor, Thomas Mundy. Mundy explained that he also was involved in the Griffiths case, and since legal action was expected soon he would be appreciative if the grand jury would wait until he had taken care of that before being called back to delve again into the Stuart mystery. Jurors agreed, but before they went home they had one more task: they wanted to see for themselves the videotape of the lineup at which Chuck allegedly identified Willie Bennett as the man who looked "most like" the gunman who had assaulted him and Carol.

As it turned out, the grand jury gave Mundy plenty of time; the group did not meet again for twenty days. And then it would be only another short session.

*   *   *

After the series of revelations beginning with Chuck's death and ending with Michael's admission that Chuck had talked to him about killing Carol, the whole city seemed exhausted. It was not only the grand jury that wanted a break. While reporters tried valiantly to keep the furnace stoked, they were running out of coal. The *Globe* published its blockbuster profiles on Carol and Chuck, both by writer Sally Jacobs, on consecutive Sundays (Carol on January 21; Chuck on January 28), but neither piece added substantially to the body of knowledge. As they say in the newsroom, they didn't move the story forward very much. The article on Carol was sycophantic, but it would have been hard to write an incisive, controversial story about a young pregnant woman killed before her prime, an apparent innocent victim whose only sin had been loving her husband too much.

The article on Chuck, however, was anything but fawning. It was, in fact, noticeably mean-spirited, apparently designed to conform to the author's idea of narcissistic behavior. It was, however, what the public wanted to hear. No one seemed to be in the mood to listen to a repetition of the glowing terms in which Chuck had been described in stories soon after the shooting. Although every accused is entitled to an advocate, Sally Jacobs was not going to be Chuck's.

Even the political front was relatively quiet. Mayor Flynn, the *Globe* noted in a January 19 story (another of those that lodged in the gray area separating analysis from news), might be hurting himself politically by maintaining his loyalty to Police Commissioner Roache.

And Attorney General James Shannon, who also had come under some light fire as a result of the Bennett/Stuart situation, seemed to be trying to clear his name by announcing that his office would investigate Dereck Jackson's and Eric Whitney's allegations of police intimidation.

Boston news junkies, accustomed to much more lively fare in the last couple of months, stifled a collective yawn.

Another flare-up of crime stories began on January 17 when Mark Belmore, a nineteen-year-old white student at Northeastern University, was accosted on the street soon after leaving his girlfriend's dorm and, despite loud screams for assistance, was brutally beaten and stabbed to death. The incident occurred on the fringe of Mission Hill, not far from where Chuck said he and Carol were stopped. There was more than one reference to the fact that Belmore, a husky sophomore who aspired to be a federal marshal, was killed by a black gang in retaliation for what had been done to Willie Bennett.

Adding drama to the case was much finger pointing and hand wringing by the city's news organizations, which said police conspired to keep Belmore's murder a secret. They theorized that the murder was hushed up because it had occurred on Martin Luther King, Jr., Day, and the assailants appeared to be several black youths. Authorities were said to fear that if it had been announced on the country's only holiday honoring a black civil rights leader that a group of blacks were believed responsible for a possible racially motivated killing in Roxbury, it would exacerbate the already tense situation. However, less than a week later, three black youths, including teenaged twin brothers, were arrested and charged with Mark Belmore's death. The fears that the city's blacks would be outraged by the arrests and use them to renew accusations of racial discrimination proved groundless.

The incident, though, said something about problems among the city's news organizations. One veteran media watcher, reading details in the *Globe* about how police allegedly hid the details when they were contacted by reporters, shook his head sadly. "You know what that says?" he asked. "It says the *Globe*, even after all that has happened, is still covering the police department by telephone."

While residents of Boston appeared weary (and wary) of more revelations, the Stuart case would not go away, certainly not while there were so many questions still to be answered. On January 16 the local NBC affiliate, WBZ-TV, on its noon talk show, *People Are Talking*, examined the issue through the eyes of some of the reporters who covered it. The television newsrooms were represented, with the exception of WNEV (CBS), which was mysteriously absent. A WBZ radio reporter was there, along with Ellen Hume, a former reporter for the *Los Angeles Times* and now executive director of the Joan Shorenstein Barone Center on the Press, Politics and Public Policy at Harvard, and Alan Dershowitz, a controversial and outspoken professor from Harvard Law School. Both the *Globe* and the *Herald* declined to take part.

The most remarkable thing to come out of the program was the lack of concrete information. For a case so far advanced, there was still much that was not known. As Ron Golobin, news director at WCVB-TV (ABC), pointed out dryly, even then no one could say with any certainty who had shot Carol or Chuck, exactly when it had happened, where it had happened, or why. "The only thing we know for sure is that the shooting did *not* occur while Chuck was on the line with McLaughlin," Golobin said. "Otherwise we would have heard the shots."

Charles Austin, an articulate and soft-spoken reporter from WBZ-TV, said one of the things that amazed him about the case was how many people knew or had reason to suspect from the beginning that Chuck had been involved. He ticked them off. There was Matthew, of course, he said, and Jack McMahon. There was Michael, who not only had been told by Matthew but had had a conversation with Chuck in which Chuck had talked about Carol's murder. There was David MacLean. And later, even before Matthew went to the authorities, the rest of the Stuart siblings knew, as did Chuck's parents. Attorneys Clayman and Perenyi knew something was up, and Jay Kakas, who probably should have thought of looking in the company safe to see if the snub-nosed, nickel-plated .38-caliber weapon he had bought years before was still there, may have had at least a strong suspicion.

Dershowitz raised an intriguing question, another that has never been answered. In preparing his presentation for the grand jury the previous November, had ADA Mundy planned to call Chuck to testify? Or Matthew? Or, Janet Monteforte, Matthew's girlfriend at the time? By Christmas, with the grand jury still out, both Matthew and Monteforte had talked to Perenyi. If they had been called before the grand jury between then and January 3, when Matthew went to authorities, they would have had three choices. They could have claimed protection against self-incrimination under the Fifth Amendment and said nothing. They could have lied, in which case Perenyi would have been obligated to come forward. Or they could have told the truth, in which case the investigation would have blown open sooner than it did.

There also was comment about Bennett, who, they agreed, seemed a not unreasonable suspect, especially in light of his long record. A voice from the background drifted into a microphone. "He doesn't have a record," the voice said, "he has an album."

Ironically, two weeks later Bennett was back into the case. On January 31 reporters discovered a document that had been filed by District Attorney Flanagan, who earlier had said that Bennett was no longer a suspect in the Stuart shooting.

The document was part of a bulky legal brief filed by Flanagan's office in opposition to a request from WBZ-TV for a copy of the videotape of the lineup at which Chuck allegedly fingered Bennett as the man who looked "most like" the mysterious assailant. Signed by ADA Mundy, the document argued that the videotape should not be released to WBZ because "the man reportedly identified in the lineup may yet turn out to have some connection with the case." It did not specify what the "connection" might be.

Chapter 20

One day when everything has been settled in this case, or as settled as it is likely to get, someone will be able to look at it unemotionally and study it without the tensions that have made the name "Stuart" so controversial. Perhaps they will determine that much of the sharp criticism leveled against police and the district attorney's office for their early handling of the situation was not altogether fair. Although they hardly covered themselves with glory, they probably did not act as unprofessionally as some have indicated. Disregarding the likelihood that high-ranking police officials used poor judgment in flooding Mission Hill with officers, or that they unwisely put into operation the questionable stop-and-search tactics that already were under attack, the assumptions police made at the beginning were not unreasonable. Chuck's story *was* credible. Mission Hill *was* a high-crime area. He and Carol *were* likely victims. His description of the assailant was detailed and un-wavering. There was nothing on the surface to indicate that he would want to kill his wife. And one of the most compelling arguments of all was the seriousness of Chuck's wound. If a man planned to kill his wife and then wound himself to make it look as though someone else had attacked the two of them, he would want to make sure that he did not kill himself in the process. But Chuck Stuart almost died. Investigators must have thought about that a lot as they paced the grim corridors at BCH waiting to see if they were going to be able to talk to Chuck or if he was going to succumb to his wound before he could give them any pertinent information.

Police later admitted, grudgingly, that they did not consider Chuck a suspect until Matthew came forward, that they never searched his home or dug too deeply into his past. Part of the criticism centers around the fact that police should have adhered to the rule that says when a wife is killed the husband must always be the prime suspect. Without having many of the details that were available to police in those first days, such as lab reports, early witness interviews, and details on the investigators assigned to the case (how experienced were they? were they veteran homicide detectives? had they seen much domestic violence?), it is difficult to make a judgment about what they should have seen or surmised. Certainly there appeared to be nothing in the physical realm to raise their suspicions. As for the accusation that police ignored reporters' attempts to make them look at Chuck more closely, so what? Police accept journalists' advice on how to conduct investigations about as enthusiastically as journalists accept police advice on how to run their newsrooms. As has been shown, the media did not have all the answers, either. Nor do they yet.

If there is a real weak spot in the way the police handled the case in its developmental stages, it is in the timing of the lineup. Chuck was released from BCH on December 5, but the lineup was not held until December 23, which was an unusually long time to let such a function hang fire. Just why there was such a long delay is, not surprisingly, unclear. Mundy, the chief prosecutor in the case, has said that delays were requested by Bennett's attorneys. However, the two attorneys who represented Bennett during that period have said that was not true. According to *them*, Stuart had been out of the hospital for ten days before the district attorney's office even mentioned the possibility of a lineup.

Critics of the police claim the long delay helped set up the situation under which Chuck was almost certain to pick Bennett as the one who looked "most like" his attacker. For one thing, they say, Chuck's memory undoubtedly dulled during the long interval between the attack on October 23 and the lineup on December 23, making him more susceptible to error in identifying his assailant, assuming there *was* an assailant. For another, since Chuck was out of the hospital and there was no one to assure that he did not comb the newspapers or flip through the newscasts to see what he could learn about the man everyone said was the prime suspect in the shooting, there was nothing to prevent him from having seen a picture of Bennett, either in one of the newspapers or on television.

There are, however, two potential problems with that theory. One, the two pictures of Bennett that received the most play (and possibly the only ones) were a shot of him taken over his shoulder in which his coat collar was raised to cover three-fourths of his face and a grainy profile shot that revealed next to nothing of his features. In a section of film footage he was even less visible since he wore a stocking cap pulled down to his eyebrows and kept the lower part of his face hidden with his coat collar.

A second problem was that police have not said what steps Bennett may have taken either just before or just after his arrest to alter his appearance. When Chuck originally described his assailant, he said the man wore his hair in a short afro and sported a patchy beard. But in the pictures of Bennett taken at his arraignment on November 13, his head was close-cropped and his cheeks were clean-shaven; the only facial hair was a hint of a mustache.

There was one other interesting development as well. A story in the *Globe* on January 9 reported that employees of a video store in Brookline that allegedly was robbed by Bennett on October 2 had to be shown two sets of Bennett's pictures before they made an identification. The first set of pictures were apparently old shots of Bennett, and when they were shown to the employees, who presumably got a much better look at the robber than Chuck did of his alleged assailant, they said they were not sure that he was the holdup man. Then, when officers came back a week later with color pictures of Bennett taken after he was arrested on November 11, they made a positive identification.

There was one other thing, too, that more than likely helped influence Chuck's identification of Willie Bennett. The district attorney's office admitted that Bennett was the only person whose photo was shown to Chuck while he was in the hospital and who also appeared later in the lineup. Under those conditions, when Chuck saw Bennett in the lineup he undoubtedly looked familiar because he had already seen his photo in two separate groups of pictures that had been shown to him in November. Criminal justice experts call that a "photo-biased identification"; it is a definite no-no if investigators expect an identification to stand up later in a courtroom.

However, according to Mundy, Chuck had already had a strong response to Bennett's picture even before he saw him in the lineup. According to the ADA, Bennett was one of two people Chuck picked from an initial set of pictures of possible suspects shown him soon after Bennett's arrest. Some ten days later a second group of pictures was shown to Chuck that also included pictures of Bennett. When Chuck picked up the picture of Bennett, his hand began shaking violently enough to prompt the investigator to ask him why he was so upset. Chuck replied: "This is the best photograph I've seen so far."

He was shown no more pictures by police before he went into the lineup.

* * *

Although the district attorney's office has never been effusive with information about how it handled the case, late in January ADA Mundy spoke candidly about some of the details covering not only Chuck, but the circumstances that led to the arrest of Willie Bennett. Obviously eager to defend the office against the charges of intimidation leveled by Dereck Jackson and Eric Whitney, Mundy contended that their credibility was never under serious attack until they went back to the grand jury to recant their earlier testimony. The reason, he said, was that both youths had used the magic words that seemed to indicate they knew what they were talking about. Both quoted Willie Bennett as having said that he told Chuck, when he got into Carol's Toyota, "Don't look in the rearview mirror." The fact that those exact words had been accredited to the assailant was known only to police, to Chuck, and to the alleged assailant.

The prosecutor added that when he met with the youths in November before they testified for the first time before the grand jury, both gave detailed descriptions of what Bennett had said. Further strengthening the prosecution case was the fact that investigators had statements from other witnesses that implicated Bennett and dovetailed with what the two youths had said. One woman, identified as Mary Smith, had said that she saw Bennett sometime between eight and eleven P.M. with a nickel-plated pistol in his hand. The spot where Chuck and Carol was found was less than 150 yards from where Mary Smith said she saw Bennett. However, as she described him, the man she saw was not wearing a black jogging suit. Many weeks later Mary Smith would join Dereck Jackson and Eric Whitney in recanting her testimony. In February, contradicting what she had said in November, Mary Smith said she was coerced by police into giving her statement incriminating Bennett.

There was, however, still another witness, a second woman, Tony Jackson. According to a police affidavit, she said that she had heard Bennett implicate himself. According to her, she saw Bennett pounding a wall in frustration. When she asked him what was the matter, he allegedly said, "The bullet was not meant for the lady; it was meant for the man."

Also, at that stage of the investigation no one was focusing on Chuck as a possible suspect. Even when Mundy made these statements, late in January almost three weeks after Chuck's death, the ADA said he still had no idea what Chuck's motive may have been in wanting to kill his wife. "We don't know any more today than we did on January 4," he told the *Herald*'s Charles Craig. "Nothing has been brought to us now that should have been obvious." Despite the advantages of hindsight, the prosecutor confessed that investigators had not seen any arrows pointing toward Chuck.

"As unusual as it might seem for a mugger to jump in the backseat of a car and shoot two people who probably didn't get a good look at him," Craig quoted Mundy as saying, "it pales by comparison for someone who makes $105,000 [sic] a year; whose only vice is playing hockey on Wednesday nights; who likes to go to sporting events with friends; who works fifty-two hours a week; whose wife makes $50,000 [sic] a year; and who friends said was enthralled with his wife and baby—it appears to me beyond belief that he would shoot her and shoot himself and claim they were robbed."

The major factors pointing *against* Chuck as the gunman, Mundy emphasized, were the seriousness of his wound and the fact that no gun was found either in the car or anywhere in the vicinity. He frowned. "Who could have expected the diabolical fiend made arrangements for someone to come by and get the gun to make it look like a robbery?"

Chapter 21

The Stuart case was unique, and in large part because of this uniqueness it was an extremely difficult story to tell. The ways the media chose to tell the story were unique, too. Not because they wanted to, but because they had to. The Stuart case brought about some very unusual conditions that were forced upon the media; to survive they had to adapt. To cover the rapid developments in the case, they had to vary considerably from their normal routines; they had to adopt new methods and new avenues. Sometimes they succeeded, sometimes they did not. Whatever else may transpire with this case, it almost certainly will become a study to be pondered and debated for years in journalism schools and media think tanks.

The biggest obstacle the media faced in trying to cover developments in the case was a complete dearth of official cooperation. Pick up any newspaper or listen carefully to any newscast and one common strain can be ascertained: 99.8 percent of all the stories (excluding opinion or human-interest pieces) printed or broadcast contain some type of attribution. That is, the point being made in the particular story can be attributed specifically to some person, some group, or some document. This is what was so noticeably, and pitiably, lacking in the Stuart case. Less than a week after Carol and Chuck were shot, officials effectively shut their doors to reporters. The very first story the *Globe* wrote on the case on October 24 attributed the basic information contained therein to Boston Police Deputy Superintendent Joseph Dunford. His name never appeared again. Other early stories quoted Boston Police Superintendent Joseph V. Saia, Jr., but within three or four days his name also disappeared. In less than a week no one in an official capacity was willing to talk on the record to reporters.

Of course, this did not mean that some of the sources were not keeping lines of communication open to the media. But they had decided, seemingly in unison, that they would no longer speak for attribution. This meant that reporters were forced to use weak identifiers such as "sources," "investigators," "someone close to the investigation," "unnamed police department official," and so forth. What this did was deprive readers and listeners of the opportunity of evaluating what they were being told. Information may still have been coming from Saia, for example, who because of his job presumably had available to him reports from throughout the department and could make intelligent judgments about the status of the investigation, an advantage that was not available to the cop on the beat. Yet when a development was said to have occurred and reporters attributed this new information to "a police department source," the public did not know if it came from Saia or rookie patrolman Mickey Murphy.

A good example was an incident surrounding the arrest of Alan Swanson, the first publicly announced suspect in the shooting. Police went to arrest Swanson not because they considered him a suspect in the Stuart shooting, but because he allegedly was squatting in someone else's apartment. But when officers burst in to arrest him, one went into the bathroom. There, soaking in a plastic pail, was a black jogging suit. Aware that Chuck Stuart had said that the man who attacked him and his wife had been wearing a black jogging suit, the officer jumped to a conclusion. Convinced that Swanson had suddenly turned into a hot suspect as the Stuart gunman, the cop immediately went to a judge seeking a warrant to make a thorough search of the apartment. Since he had to have a good reason for getting such a warrant, he exaggerated a bit. In his request to the judge, he did not say he had found *a* black jogging suit that was similar to the one worn by the alleged attacker in the Stuart case; he said he had uncovered *the* sweatsuit worn by the man who had killed Carol Stuart. The warrant was granted, but no other evidence implicating Swanson was found. However, the point was that one relatively low ranking police officer had made a very bad assumption. Unfortunately a reporter compounded the error. Soon there was a TV news report saying that police had found the jogging suit worn by Carol Stuart's killer and a suspect had been taken into custody. If the information about the jogging suit had gone higher up the line before a request had been filed with the judge, someone more discriminating might have said, "Hey, we're not saying this is *the* jogging suit, but one that looks like the garment described by the victim." The difference is subtle but significant.

This type of thing may have made a difference in the early days. Later it ceased to matter because official sources took the easy way out: they simply clammed up. And this made a huge difference in the way the public was informed about developments in the case. It paved the way for such apparent major errors as the report that Chuck was treated for drug addiction at Boston City Hospital and that Chuck had been scheduled to collect on his wife's $480,000 insurance policy on the day he died. No one except the reporters who filed those reports knows from whence they came. But if someone in authority had been willing to come forward and say definitively that Chuck did *not* undergo treatment for addiction or that there was *no* $480,000 policy, those two claims might have been stopped before they were made public. Curiously, the two newspapers involved, the *Herald* in the detox story and the *Globe* in the insurance policy piece, are standing by their claims despite the denials. Both are taking the position that time will prove these stories true. Who knows? They may be right. In this case, stranger things have happened.

Even before the new grand jury began delving in any depth into the tangled circumstances, attempts were being made to analyze media coverage of the story. On television, the first such attempt was the *People Are Talking* segment on Boston's WBZ-TV. However, it dealt not so much with *how* the media covered the story, but with the nitty-gritty of the story itself. Interestingly, though, at the very beginning of the program, when host Tom Bergeron asked the assembled newspeople how many of them suspected early on that Chuck was involved in the shooting, all except one raised his hand. Although not a single newspaper or radio or television station allowed these suspicions to creep into print or on the air, either as news or commentary, it may help explain the alacrity with which the Boston media later accepted, at least as unquestionably as they had accepted the first story, the contention that Chuck shot Carol and himself and later committed suicide.

Interestingly, in the days since Chuck's death, some Boston reporters have said privately that they think the scenario may not turn out to be exactly as it has been painted, but again these doubts were not printed or aired. If, by chance, the grand jury happened to come back and say that events did not transpire at all the way they had been depicted in the newspapers and on the air in January and February, reporters could again say that they knew it all along. Why such doubts—and unquestionably some do exist—have not been made public is anybody's guess.

While the *People Are Talking* show dealt mainly with the mechanics of the Stuart case coverage, a soon-to-follow special on WCVB-TV, the ABC affiliate, emphasized policy. Produced by a television division of the Columbia University Graduate

School of Journalism called Media and Society, the program was taped in Boston on January 17, the day after the *People Are Talking* segment was aired, but it was not shown until January 25. Entitled "The Boston Hoax," the program was literally a round table debate on how the media had performed up until then. The host for the program was Fred Friendly, former president of *CBS News* and currently professor emeritus at Columbia.

The show had a large and varied panel, which was both its blessing and its curse. For the first time on the air, the people who made the decisions about the Stuart coverage at the opposing Boston newspapers sat at the same table: Greg Moore, an assistant managing editor at the *Globe*, and Kenneth Chandler, the editor of the *Herald*. Other newspeople on the show were Emily Rooney, news director at WCVB; one of her reporters, David Ropeik; and Charles Austin, a reporter at WBZ-TV, who also had been on the *People Are Talking* program. The rest of the group was diverse. There was Bill Kovach, former Washington bureau chief for *The New York Times*, former editor of the *Atlanta Constitution*, and currently curator of the Nieman Fellowship program at Harvard; Dianne Wilkerson, an attorney for the Boston chapter of the NAACP; District Attorney Newman Flanagan; and Dr. Alvin F. Poussaint, an associate professor of psychiatry at the Harvard Medical School (which is only a few blocks from where the October 23 drama was played out). Poussaint specializes in race relations and is a regular on the talk show circuit.

The idea for the panel was a good one; in theory it provided a venue for examination of a case that, as Friendly said, was so extraordinary that it would never have been accepted by a panel if it had been presented as hypothetical. In practice, however, the panel failed in its objective because the group was too large and too many people had their own agendas. Poussaint and Wilkerson wanted to promote the case as an example of how blacks are discriminated against in news coverage, as well as how editors and news directors use crime coverage to perpetuate stereotypes of blacks as law violators. Flanagan wanted to cover his back and take his shots at the newspapers. Kovach wanted to talk about media responsibility in the general sense, particularly how virtually all organizations are doing a poor job of covering the inner cities. And the editors, reporters, and news director wanted to explain and defend their coverage.

A good bit of the early part of the show—too much, in fact—was taken up with a discussion of the *Herald*'s decision to print on its front page a graphic photograph taken on the night of the shooting. The picture, which was later printed in *Time* magazine without the charge of yellow journalism leveled at the *Herald*'s Chandler, showed Chuck and Carol before they were extricated from their car. Taken from the front of the car through the windshield, it offered a full-face view of Carol slumped on her seat, her chin on her chest and her mouth sagging open. Chuck was shown rigid in pain, his shirt ripped away with his chest and stomach exposed. Both Moore and Rooney said their organizations had access to the picture and declined to use it because they thought it violated the victims' privacy. When asked why he'd made the decision to use the picture, Chandler said simply, "We're not in the business of suppressing news."

Wilkerson took a somewhat baffling position. She said she abhorred the picture so much that she still had not forced herself to take a good look at it. But even while castigating Chandler for using the photo, she claimed that the *Herald*, because of its racial bias, would never have used a similar picture of black crime victims.

Poussaint had a one-track argument: that the coverage given the Stuart shooting reflected the racism inherent in the country's news organizations. Would the same interest have been shown in the story if the victims had been black? Probably not, he concluded, bolstering his argument that it is an accepted truism that a white life is more valuable than a black life. This also was a somewhat bewildering position to take in this case because Moore, who directed the Stuart coverage for the *Globe*, is black, as is WBZ's Charles Austin.

Flanagan was not as interested in theory as he was in specifics. Wearing his characteristic outrageous tie, this time a neon blue number with an ostentatious design that looked like a palm tree rooted in a sandbar, Flanagan contended in a heavy New England accent that news organizations are driven by one objective: selling newspapers and advertising; therefore the more they can hype a story, the better it is for business. This is a common accusation made by those with little understanding of how a newsroom operates. Although the *Herald* relies heavily on newsstand sales, its future is not determined by the appeal of a single issue, nor will its solvency be determined by whether it prints or does not print a specific photograph. Although Flanagan and other critics are correct when they say that the aim of a newspaper or a television station is to make money, he and the other critics are dead wrong when they say that the issue is uppermost in the minds of those who make the everyday news decisions. Line editors, news directors, and reporters are too wrapped up in the technicalities of covering events to give more than a passing thought to the economic realities of the industry. That is what publishers and owners are for. In this case, the workaday journalists were too concerned with the rapidly changing dynamics of the Stuart story to consider its impact on the cash flow.

Many critics seem to think that the need to make a profit is the engine that drives a news operation. In reality, it is the opposite: it is the integrity of the news-gathering force that drives the economics. A wise (and financially successful) publisher or owner is a salesman for the product delivered by his news crew rather than the other way around. A rough analogy, in Flanagan's context, would be to accuse the district attorney's office of drumming up crimes so the staff could perpetuate their jobs.

The other point Flanagan wanted to make was to claim unequivocally that no one on his staff had been the source for leaks about developments in the Stuart case. He did *not* say, and neither did anyone on the panel call him on it, that his office had not cooperated by releasing information that it could easily have disseminated without damaging its legal position should the issue later get into court.

Chapter 22

Newspaper analysis of media coverage in the Stuart case assumed a completely different format. While the electronic media lends itself toward panels and group discussions, newspaper analysis is performed virtually exclusively by a single person, most often by someone who has not been directly involved in the issue being analyzed.

Perhaps the first such article examining the print media's role appeared on January 8, only a little more than seventy-two hours after Chuck's body was recovered from the Mystic River. Intriguingly, the article was printed not in a Boston publication, but in *The Washington Post*. The author, Christopher B. Daly, a former Associated Press staffer in Boston, dealt more with the newspapers' defense of their actions than with an interpretation of the coverage. Still, it was fascinating on several counts.

For one thing, Daly made an early and direct connection between the Stuart case and the Ta-

wana Brawley case in upstate New York, even if it
was just a passing reference. What Daly was able
to do, however, was get immediately to the top
people at the *Globe* and the *Herald*, which was not
an inconsiderable accomplishment considering
that at the time he wrote the article the story was
still developing. *Globe* editor John Driscoll, sounding more than a little defensive, especially so early
in the evolution of the story, claimed his reporters'
coverage had been "accurate, thorough, fair, and
consistent." Furthermore, he added, the *Globe*'s
stories had been based on "official statements and
credible sources."

Either Driscoll had not spent much time in the
newsroom in those early days, or he did not want
to admit to a writer for an out-of-town newspaper
that his newspaper had tended a tad toward the
hysterical. As far as "official statements" go, the
only official statement alluded to in the *Globe* in
the January 5–8 period is the one from Flanagan
that said Willie Bennett was no longer a suspect.
By "credible sources," he had to mean Matthew's
lawyer, John Perenyi, who was the only source of
consequence, except for Flanagan, Bennett's lawyer, and the civil rights leaders, whose names appeared. Unless, of course, he was including columnist Mike Barnicle as well, the writer whose
information in a front-page personal-opinion column on January 7 also turned up in the lead story
of the day, which boasted three bylines: Kevin
Cullen, Anthony Flint, *and* Mike Barnicle. Neither
did Driscoll mention the January 5 banner headline
that proclaimed Chuck both a suicide and a wife
killer.

At the *Herald*, editor Kenneth Chandler denied that his reporters had been taken in by Chuck's original story. When his people took their suspicions to police and prosecutors, Chandler said, they were rebuffed. he also said that Matthew decided to go to authorities only after reading in the newspapers that Chuck had blamed an innocent man. "I don't think the media has anything to be ashamed of," he told Daly.

The second out-of-towner to weigh in was Alex S. Jones of *The New York Times*. His lengthy article, which appeared on January 14, seemed to be half news story and half opinion, even though it was not labeled analysis and did not appear on the op-ed page. In the news portion of the story, Jones talked to most of the people whom Daly had interviewed or who would soon be on the Columbia University special or WBZ's *People Are Talking:* the *Globe*'s Driscoll, Harvard's Poussaint and Ellen Hume, and Kovach.

Jones's story was different in one respect: it called Chuck's death an *apparent* suicide and carefully said that *the authorities identified him as the likely killer*. This, of course, was in sharp contrast with how the Boston media, except for the *Phoenix*, were characterizing Chuck.

In what appeared to be opinion, Jones noted: "Few of the reports included such usual qualifications as 'apparently' or 'said to be,' as there seemed to be no reason to think that a man who almost died of a stomach wound would lie."

But that was in the early stages of the story.

Later the media completely changed its pace. Jones wrote: "Since Mr. Stuart's death, critics say news organizations have gone to the other extreme, spewing a torrent of information about the case based on anonymous sources in what many see as a desperate overcompensation for having been fooled."

Chuck's apparent suicide may have made the media rethink its stance and decide to be more aggressive. At that point (although some think it was considerably earlier), relations between the media and authorities cooled to the point of freezing. Jones said: "Stung by criticism that they had not been sufficiently aggressive, Boston's news organizations shifted to the other extreme, began reporting everything, and were immediately denounced for hindering the investigation."

In the beginning, Jones pointed out, the Boston media was criticized for not being skeptical enough of authorities, but after Chuck's death critics jumped on them for not being skeptical enough of their anonymous sources. To emphasize this point, Jones quoted Ellen Hume: "Journalists are supposed to keep cool heads in the midst of the crisis, and I don't think they've done that as they fall over themselves to correct their own behavior."

These were harsh words, but they were going to get harsher. In three long articles over as many weeks, *Boston Phoenix* media critic Mark Jurkowitz chastised the two Boston dailies as well as some of the other newspapers and magazines that reported on the case. On January 12, beating the *Times* into print, Jurkowitz wrote a day-by-day critique of how the Boston papers reacted to Chuck's death and the other related events. Overall, he said, the result was chaotic.

"In the days since Chuck's death turned the Stuart murder story completely on its head, revisionist history has been written at a frantic pace, scapegoating has become the local pastime, and rumors have been flying faster than the Concorde."

Jurkowitz somewhat gleefully pointed out the obvious errors and even more gleefully swung a few punches at Mike Barnicle. At one point he noted how the columnist had used an unnamed source to break the news that Chuck had tried to kill his wife earlier. This leaves "the reader to judge [the report's] believability depending largely on how he or she feels about Barnicle." He did not leave much doubt about how *he* felt about Barnicle.

Scoring each day's coverage as a judge would tally rounds in a prizefight, Jurkowitz decided that at the end of the first week the *Globe* had edged the *Herald* three rounds to two, with one round as a tie. "But," he concluded, "because the *Globe*'s big rounds were bigger than the *Herald*'s big rounds, I'd score it 58–55 *Globe*."

In his February 2 column Jurkowitz took after Barnicle in full force, reminding *Phoenix* readers how, three years previously, the columnist had created a minicrisis by writing about a prostitute allegedly infected with AIDS who was deliberately spreading the disease among her clients. When authorities found the woman, Jurkowitz said, she tested negative for the disease.

Two years before that, he added, Barnicle had seriously garbled the facts when he wrote a column allegedly detailing how a woman riding on the subway had overheard a man bragging about shooting a young woman, who was the subway rider's daughter. That incident, he added, caused the *Globe* considerable embarrassment.

And there was one more dig. "There are plenty of folks," Jurkowitz wrote, "who feel Barnicle has basically functioned as a shill for the beleaguered Boston cops on the Stuart story."

The closest to self-criticism performed by either of the two dailies came from the *Globe* in a column by ombudsman Robert L. Kierstead. Although the column appeared primarily to be a venue for *Globe* higher-ups to excuse away their lapses, Kierstead, in his conclusion, gave the paper the mildest of taps on the wrist. The same person who had been writing the headlines for the main stories must have been doing heads for the op-ed page that day as well because the title over the column supported earlier contentions that Chuck was a narcissist and/ or a sociopath. A STORY WEAVED BY "A WORLD-CLASS CON MAN," it read.

In the article Kierstead related how the *Globe*'s Sunday managing editor, Al Larkin, claimed he knew on October 24, the morning after the shooting, that Chuck was the perpetrator. His reasons for suspecting Chuck, he told the ombudsman, were the route Chuck decided to take to leave the city, the fact that the intersection where Chuck said he was accosted was too busy to make such an abduction plausible, and Chuck's apparent lack of concern for Carol, as evidenced by his conversation with Gary McLaughlin.

The column also stressed the claims by *Globe* editors that they tried hard to shoot down Chuck's story. "When we heard rumors, we checked them out," said Assistant Managing Editor Greg Moore, the man in charge of coordinating the Stuart coverage. "They continued virtually unabated, but every one led to a dead end."

In the weeks before January 4, Larkin said, reporters investigated Chuck's background as well as they could. "We checked his status on drugs, on money, possible marital difficulties, insurance policies, whether he had a gun, a gun permit, was he familiar with the Mission Hill area, was he flirting with the BCH nurses." But, added Editor Driscoll, the more reporters checked, the better Chuck looked. "Our thinking of Stuart as the killer began diminishing as each day went by. This was due partly to his reputation and partly because the rumors, one after the other, were found to be erroneous. But mostly [not much was discovered] because we were being conned by a world-class con man."

Peter Mancusi, the *Globe*'s city editor, also beat his breast. "We were all skeptical of Stuart's story," he said. "For months we chased all the rumors out there. We talked to dozens who knew Chuck or might have information about him. We couldn't put a dent in his story. You can't print rumors, so we couldn't get anything in the paper to shoot down his story."

After listening to these arguments (and printing them for posterity), Kierstead decided that his colleagues, despite what they had said, perhaps did not check quite hard enough. But his criticism did not ring sufficiently sincere, especially not after he added, in his colleagues' defense, that they had been dealing with a "diabolically clever" man, who, "regardless of his very serious wound, could so totally elude the probes of both law enforcement officials and the media for more than ten weeks."

Kierstead seemed to regard the Willie Bennett incident as a separate issue, and although he did not elaborate upon the reasons for his conclusions, he wrote: "The *Globe* should have dug harder on its own into the Willie Bennett part of the story, despite what the police believed was a seemingly good case against him."

The electronic media got by easier than their print colleagues, at least as far as volume of criticism. That is because media criticism in Boston is the exclusive purview of the newspapers. But the Boston broadcasters took their lumps, too. Terry Ann Knopf, TV editor for the Quincy *Patriot Ledger*, delivered a stinging column on January 19 that attacked both print and broadcast reporters, but especially the broadcasters.

"The rush to piece together the story has resulted in some of the shoddiest newspaper and TV reporting in memory," she wrote, specifically citing WCBV's Jack Harper (for using an unsubstantiated figure on the amount of insurance Chuck had on his wife, which preceded Barnicle's apparent error by a week) and WBZ anchor Jack Williams (who bragged prematurely that results of the FBI tests would be available the next day).

A WBZ special on the Stuart case on January 17

(the day after the *People Are Talking* show and eight days before the Columbia University program, which she called "ho-hum") came in for special attention. "The first half was a tired rehash," Knopf wrote, and in the second half anchors Williams and Liz Walker "missed a golden opportunity to grill Richard Clayman," who called a news conference some twelve hours later for his blockbuster announcement that Michael was aware of Chuck's involvement.

Chapter 23

Carol's parents, the DiMaitis, retreated into seclusion with their grief the day after Chuck's body was found. On January 25, exactly three weeks after Chuck allegedly committed suicide, three months and one day after their daughter died, Giusto and Evelyn, with their son, Carl, at their side, announced the creation of the Carol DiMaiti Stuart Foundation, a nonprofit organization whose primary purpose would be to provide college financial aid for Mission Hill students.

Fighting back tears, an exhausted-looking Giusto tried to put his family's anguish into words. Evelyn, clad in a plain dark dress and looking even more distraught than her husband, dabbed gently around her distress-darkened eyes while her husband read haltingly from a typewritten sheet.

"Our daughter was truly the brightest of lights in our lives, a light that will never go out in our minds," he read. "Her mother and I are filled with pride for the way she lived her life. She brought joy and comfort, not only to us, but to all she knew. Carol was a loving, caring person who always thought of the other person first. She loved to help those less fortunate than herself and was constantly trying to improve their place in this world by donating her legal skills to them and helping them in any way she could. She will always and forever be with us. We pray that God has taken her and our beloved grandson, Christopher, into his embrace in heaven, where they will be safe and happy with Him until the time we will join them."

Looking somewhat embarrassed, he apologized to the assembled reporters for what he seemed to consider a slightly impersonal presentation. "I must ask your forgiveness in reading this statement," he said, "but I don't honestly feel I could have managed without it. It is very important for you to know that we have received expressions of sympathy from a tremendous cross section of the general public. It's amazing to realize how this tragedy has touched a large number of people. So many of you have responded in a caring and loving way. You have our deepest gratitude and love for your support and thoughtfulness in helping us through this continuing nightmare."

As Giusto stepped away from the microphone, looking as though he could not hold back the flood much longer, the DiMaitis' attorney, Marvin Geller, moved forward. Although the main purpose of the foundation would be to offer financial aid to needy students, he said, its deeper purpose was to promote better relations between the races.

"The DiMaiti family, while suffering its own anguish, is not unmindful of the fact that the events of these past few months have caused many to look within themselves to examine their own innermost feelings about race relations and the manner in which our elected officials and the media have carried out their respective responsibilities," he said in measured, courtroom-oratory tones. "Out of this debate has emerged anger and emotion. It has opened old, painful scars of racial tension. The DiMaiti family believes that Carol would not have wanted her death to be remembered as the cause of such divisiveness. She would not want to be remembered as the victim of a sensational murder, but rather as a woman who left behind a legacy of healing and compassion."

The DiMaitis' gesture drew praise from all political and racial factions, and within hours contributions began pouring in. After five days the fund had built to $42,000, and in less than a month it had climbed to more than $250,000.

Chuck's siblings, with the exception of Matthew, watched the news conference in their lawyer's office. Afterward they declined to meet with reporters but issued a statement through Richard Clayman.

"They understand the great tragedy that has befallen the DiMaiti family," said an uncharacteristically subdued Clayman. "They understand the tremendous grief. They applaud the formation of the foundation, and I got the distinct impression they hope this will be a stepping stone to healing wounds."

The wounds Clayman was referring to apparently went beyond the normal tension that could be expected between the family of the murdered, Carol, and the accused murderer, Chuck. A fight over money also was looming on the horizon.

Just hours before the news conference that was called to announce the creation of the foundation, a lawyer representing the DiMaitis filed a petition in probate court in Middlesex County asking that Carol's brother, Carl, be named administrator of her estate. Less than a week later, Judge Vincent F. Leahy granted the request.

It was only the first step in what could, if either family felt so inclined, lead to a long, costly, bitter battle, one that could raise a number of intriguing legal questions and drag through the courts for years.

From documents filed later, it was learned that Carol's estate consisted of $7,000 in a bank account and her share of the $70,000 equity in the couple's $238,000 home in Reading. That did not include the insurance money, which was certain to be a contentious issue whether the Stuarts and the DiMaitis are able to settle the dispute or if they have to go to court.

The amount of money apparently was not in dispute. After Carol's death, Chuck collected $82,000 on a policy she had through her employer. There were two additional $100,000 policies, bringing the total *publicly known* amount of insurance on Carol to $282,000. Chuck also had two $100,000 policies on his life and another policy, with the company for which his father once worked, for $14,000, for a total of $214,000. Since Charles Stuart was listed as the beneficiary of the smaller policy, it is not believed that amount will be at issue. Between them, though, Chuck's and Carol's insurance policies totaled at least $482,000. The tricky part will be deciding who will fall heir to that amount since both Chuck and Carol, as well as their only child, are dead.

Legal experts have speculated that if a settlement is not reached, a court will have to decide several very sensitive issues before it can be determined how the money will be divided. Normally, in a community-property state such as Massachusetts, when a mother dies without a will, as Carol did, half of her estate goes to her child or children; the other half goes to her husband.

Also under normal circumstances, if the husband then dies, his insurance money, plus his share of his wife's, would go into his estate. Since Chuck also died without a will, and since Carol and Christopher are dead, his money would go to his parents.

But this case has been anything but normal. The circumstances, in fact, make the inheritance situation very complicated. The first hurdle to be surmounted, if the issue has to go to court, is trying to determine if Chuck murdered his wife, because if he did, his estate might not be able to claim her insurance money. The second hurdle is the question about when Carol died. Apparently she was not breathing when she arrived at Brigham and Women's, although in the absence of medical reports it is difficult to say that with certainty. If she was not breathing, was she dead? She was not formally pronounced dead for several hours, but was her breathing artificially induced by life-support equipment? This is an important issue because if a court determines that Carol was already dead before Christopher was delivered by cesarean section, Chuck apparently would be the sole beneficiary. If it is determined that Carol was still alive when Christopher was born, then he would become an heir, along with Chuck. Then when he died seventeen days later, his portion of his mother's estate would be divided between Chuck, the DiMaitis, and the Stuarts.

Since Chuck can never be tried for Carol's murder, there apparently would be no official determination on that point. Also, while there is no law in Massachusetts prohibiting a spouse from collecting on a murdered partner's insurance, there is what is called a "public policy," under which spouses in such situations have been barred from collecting.

There are still some unknowns, too, which make it even more complicated. Did any or all of Carol's policies contain double-indemnity clauses? Did any or all of Chuck's policies contain clauses that prohibit payment in case of suicide? Which brings the question full circle: Did Chuck commit suicide? Did Chuck kill Carol and Christopher?

If a court has to step in and settle these questions—that is, if either the DiMaitis or the Stuarts file suit—a decision could take years. A final irony could be that if the case drags on indefinitely, either of the Stuarts, neither of whom is in good health, could die, and presumably their estate (which may then include Chuck's) could go to their children, including Michael and Matthew.

Chapter 24

On the last day of January, the new twenty-three-member grand jury impaneled specifically to hear evidence in the Stuart case met in the Suffolk County Courthouse to begin its investigation. As he had done with everything else in this case, Flanagan drew a cloak of secrecy over the group, declining even to reveal its composition by sex, race, or age. However, the district attorney could not ban reporters from the courthouse corridors, so they camped out in the hallways and kept at least a running account of who went in, if not what they said.

One of the first witnesses was Special Agent William A. Tobin, a metallurgist at the FBI Laboratory in Washington. Although reporters might not immediately recognize some of the witnesses being called before the group, particularly if they were not normally in the limelight, Tobin was readily identifiable because he was lugging a green-and-

white beer cooler. When the weapon suspected to
have been used to shoot Chuck and Carol was
recovered from the Pines River on January 9, investigators put it immediately into a container filled
with river water to help preserve it until experts
could run their tests. Even after the tests were
completed, it continued to be stored in the water
to retard deterioration as much as possible.

As if there were not enough strange coincidences
in this case, ironical connections that seemed to
pop up everywhere, the newspapers soon discovered that Tobin had a strong connection to Boston.
He had attended grammar school in nearby Bourne
when his father was stationed in the area with the
U.S. Air Force. But his ties were even stronger than
that; he had a legal connection to Boston because
of a murder case that almost equaled the Stuart
case in its luridness. In the early 1970s there were
a series of gory murders of women hitchhikers in
and around Boston. A man with a genius-level IQ
named Anthony Jackson was charged with the killings and brought to trial. During the investigation,
it had been determined that the killer had kept his
victims in closets before he killed them, nailing the
doors shut to keep them from escaping. Tobin was
brought into the case when prosecutors asked the
metallurgist to testify about the composition of the
nails used to secure the closet doors and how they
were linked to Jackson.

Jackson spent the weekend before Tobin testified
learning as much as he could about metallurgy and
then, acting as his own counsel, cross-examined the
FBI agent for two days about his conclusions.

In spite of his efforts, Jackson was convicted of

killing three of the women and was sentenced to three consecutive life sentences. Now nearing fifty, he is still behind bars.

Whether Tobin will ever testify in court in connection with the Stuart case remained up to the grand jury. Although he refused to tell reporters what he testified about behind closed doors, it almost certainly dealt with the tests he had performed on the Pines River gun. What the grand jury would need to know to help them make their decision was how long the pistol had been in the water; had it come from the safe at Kakas & Sons; whose fingerprints were on it; and was it the weapon from which the shots that killed Carol and wounded Chuck were fired.

From what Matthew had told investigators, it could be assumed that the weapon had been handled by Chuck, Matthew, and Jack McMahon, so it would not be a surprise if all three of their fingerprints were on the pistol. However, if there were a fourth set of fingerprints, the police could then deduce that there had been a third person in the car and that that person may have fired the shots.

It also was important to determine how long the gun had been in the river. According to Matthew, he took the gun from Chuck, then went to pick up McMahon, and the two of them went immediately to the river, where McMahon tossed in the pistol. If it was determined that the weapon had not been in the water as long as Matthew had indicated, then it would have to have been kept somewhere else for an undetermined period of time. If that turned out to be the case, it might prove nothing except that Matthew had lied about a small part of the story he told investigators. And if he lied about one thing, he may have lied about others.

One of the problems facing investigators, however, was the degree of accuracy of the tests being used to determine the amount of time the gun had been in the river. Several conditions, such as temperature and salt content of the water, could affect the results. If Tobin's analysis could pinpoint with reasonable accuracy the length of time the gun had been submerged, it could have an important bearing on the case.

Others testifying during the five-hour session that Wednesday were Dr. Edwin Hirsch, chief of surgery at Boston City Hospital; Peter Jaworski; and his wife, Kimberley. Both Jaworskis worked at Kakas & Sons; Peter was directly under Chuck. The Jaworskis also were friends of the Stuarts and socialized frequently with Chuck and Carol. When the Jaworskis were married not long before, Chuck was Peter's best man and Carol was Kimberley's matron of honor.

After they finished testifying, Tobin and the Jaworskis slipped out of the courthouse through a rear door to avoid reporters waiting outside. Hirsch bravely ran the gauntlet of newspeople but declined to comment on his testimony. "I'm not going to tell you anything," he said politely but firmly. "The grand jury rules are quite clear. I will not discuss anything I discussed with the grand jury." However, he did admit that his testimony had taken almost an hour.

The grand jury took the next day off but returned on Friday, February 2, with a long list of witnesses on its agenda. The first person to testify was

Chuck's younger brother, Mark, who had apparently been the only one of his three brothers who had not in some way known about Chuck's involvement before Carol was killed. Matthew, of course, had told investigators that he was deeply involved in the incident days before it occurred. Michael, the oldest after Chuck, had, according to his lawyer, known for weeks that Chuck had murder on his mind. Matthew had confirmed Chuck's involvement in a conversation with Michael within three days of the shooting. Mark, however, apparently was not aware of the situation until Michael told him, and maybe Shelly, on New Year's Day. What Mark told the grand jury, like the testimony of all the other witnesses, was unknown.

Others appearing before the group during its six-hour session included Brian Parsons, who was Chuck's best friend and the person with whom Chuck planned one day to have as his partner in a restaurant; Jack McMahon's girlfriend, Dona Rosa; McMahon's brother, Stephen; and, in an apparent repeat performance, Peter and Kimberley Jaworski.

Apparently in no hurry to complete its task and under no pressure from Flanagan or the media to do so, the grand jury did not meet again after its February 2 session for three weeks. On Friday, February 23, the group summoned three more of Chuck's siblings—brother Michael and half sisters Shelly and Neysa—and Michael's wife, Maria. The four arrived at the session together and left together. Afterward their lawyer, Richard Clayman, refused to say which of them had testified before the group or what they testified about. Those who had not testified at the February 23 session, he said, would appear before the group on February 26.

In a case that has never ceased to offer surprises, another revelation popped up on February 26. It came in the form of a ten-year-old boy who, up until then, the public had never heard of.

The boy, who was not identified, was brought before the grand jury to tell his story. And what he said was shocking. According to information later leaked to WBZ-TV, the boy, who lives in an apartment on St. Alphonsus Street, which is where Chuck and Carol were found by police and rescue workers, said he was alone in his room the night of October 23 when he heard a shot. Looking out the window, he saw a tall black man running away from a car that was stopped in the middle of the street. The man disappeared into the darkness. The implication was that it was Carol's car and that this testimony was sought to give credence to Chuck's original report that a black gunman was involved.

This was a curious development indeed. First of all, the boy was very young. Although he had told this story, according to the February 28 *Globe*, the day after the shooting, investigators had disregarded it. It was not part of the testimony police used to secure the warrant for Bennett's arrest. One of the reasons investigators apparently ignored the boy's tale was that he was said to be a special education student.

But there are other problems with the story as

well. For example, St. Alphonsus Street was where Chuck ended up after driving around lost for at least the thirteen minutes he was on the phone with Gary McLaughlin; it was *not* the spot at which he told the state police dispatcher that he and his wife were wounded. He told McLaughlin that he and Carol had been shot before he placed the 911 call and that the gunman had already fled the scene. If that were true, there would have been no third person in the car by the time Chuck drove to St. Alphonsus Street. There were no gunshots heard over the telephone while Chuck was connected to McLaughlin, so undoubtedly Chuck and Carol had already been wounded by then. Like so many other things in this case, this testimony raised many more questions than it answered.

What was even more peculiar about the boy's story is why the district attorney's office thought it was important enough to present to the grand jury. Perhaps Flanagan was operating under the theory that he would throw everything he had at the twenty-three jurors and let them sort it out. At least in a situation like that he could not be accused of withholding details from the panel. But whatever his motive, Flanagan kept it to himself, as he has with so many details in this case.

Judging by the jury's snail-paced progress, its mandate from Flanagan was very loose and certainly did not include a directive to act urgently. More than six weeks after the panel was brought together, there was no indication when it would finish its job, what other witnesses would be called, or whether any indictments would be handed up.

In the meantime Matthew apparently remained
estranged from his siblings, and his new lawyer,
Nancy Gertner, kept him well distanced from reporters.

Chapter 25

Although developments in the case were dutifully reported in the Boston media, they got very little if any mention in news reports elsewhere in the country. Sometime soon after the story's airing in the three national magazines, *Time*, *Newsweek*, and *People*, it dropped out of sight for all but those in the Boston area. But it could not stay that way indefinitely. It was too hot a story to keep out of the public consciousness for too long. On February 27, four months and three days after the shooting, it was presented again to a national audience, courtesy of the program *Rescue 911*. Producers of the program said they waited so long to show it because up until the time of Chuck's death they were negotiating with him for permission. After he died, that point became moot.

By chance, there had been a camera crew from the program riding with Boston paramedics on the night the shooting occurred. They had, in fact, been

trying for several days to find a situation worth
showing to a national audience when the Stuart
shooting occurred. What they came up with was
almost numbing in its intensity.

The program aired on February 27 and opened
with a dramatic and extremely well done re-creation of the scene in the state police "bunker,"
beginning when Gary McLaughlin took the call.
Shots of McLaughlin on the telephone, backed up
by the other two bunker personnel who were working that night, State Police Sergeant Dan Grabowski and fellow dispatcher Jack Moran, were
shown with the sound track of the original tape-
recorded conversation and an explanatory voice-
over by an unnamed narrator. Without knowing
this was a re-creation, it was almost impossible to
tell that a camera crew also had not been in the
bunker at the time. Skillfully, McLaughlin was
shown in profile much of the time, with cradling
the telephone and covering his mouth so the audience could not see from his lip movements that the
voice they were hearing was from a tape. At other
times the camera zoomed in on his eyes, which
were as tense as they must have been on the night
of the incident. McLaughlin proved to be a top-
notch actor.

The real drama, however, was reserved for the
footage actually taken at the scene. The camera
crew arrived with the paramedics, so the film,
jerkily realistic, showed workers cutting Carol's
seat belt and removing her from the car, then
laying her on the street until a gurney could be
brought over. The film showed her in profile, her
pregnancy prominent, being wheeled to the ambu-

lance. "We've got cardiac arrest here," the narrator noted as they struggled to load her into the ambulance. They had an estimated ten minutes, the disembodied voice explained, to get her to a hospital that was equipped to deliver her child if the baby was going to have a chance at survival. "She was taken to Brigham and Women's," the voice explained, "where only minutes before she had been attending childbirth classes."

After showing an exterior shot of the hospital's emergency entrance, the scene shifted to Chuck, who was being carried from the car on a stretcher covered with what appeared to be a rough, brown woolen blanket. His shirt had been cut away to expose his upper torso. His hands were crossed peacefully across his chest. Contrary to early media reports that said Chuck was unconcerned about his wife, the *Rescue 911* cameras recorded the wounded man several times asking about his wife and what her condition was. At one point, just as he was about to be put under for what would prove to be a six-hour operation, he asked again about Carol. The attending physician, concentrating on Chuck's wound, leaned over and said kindly, "We can't keep an update on her, we're taking care of you. Okay?"

Graphic scenes at the hospital showed Chuck, completely nude except for a sheet covering his genitals, being prepped for surgery. Needles were inserted into the inside of his elbows, and a mask connected to the anesthesia equipment was slipped over his nose and mouth. Just before that, as the cameras zoomed in for a close-up of his face, his lips were moving inaudibly. But two words he was trying to articulate were clearly intelligible: "my wife."

The camera moved smoothly from one gowned hospital worker to another, anonymous except for the concern and urgency reflected in their eyes. Another scene depicted physicians examining hastily taken X-rays, one of which showed a clearly identifiable and undeformed slug resting just above some partially glimpsed organ. "His wounds are very significant," a voice noted ominously. "They are life threatening."

After being wheeled into the operating room, Chuck was not shown again until, several minutes later, his lifeless body was being hauled out of the Mystic River.

Two things about the October 23 film were particularly revealing. One was the clarity of Chuck's mind, how he was aware of everything that was happening. His ability to respond quickly and intelligently was surprising. A policeman with a clipboard hovered over his head as he was being strapped into the ambulance.

"Did you see who did this? Who did this?" the officer asked excitedly.

"A black male," Chuck answered weakly but with remarkable calm.

"What did he have on? Do you remember?"

"A black jogging suit . . ."

"Any stripes on it? What color?"

Chuck's reply was inaudible to the camera. "Red?" the officer responded. Then, apparently after a nod from Chuck, "Red!"

The next question, "Did he have a mustache?" was followed by another moment of silence on the film. Then the policeman repeated what must have been Chuck's answer, "You don't remember."

At that point the door of the ambulance was closed and the camera recorded nothing further of the interrogation.

The other thing that was startling about the film was that it showed clearly the location of Chuck's wound. While hospital personnel, the district attorney's office, and the police department have refused to release any details about the injury, scenes captured by the camera, at least once in close-up, revealed that the bullet entered Chuck's body low on his right side, almost in the back, just above his kidney. It was no wonder that physicians later said they had no suspicion that Chuck's wound was self-inflicted. To have shot himself in that spot, it appears that Chuck would have to have been a contortionist.

AFTERWORD

One of the things that has made this story so compelling has been the labyrinthine but nevertheless well-defined stages of its development. It works as a good human-interest story on several levels. First there was the breathtaking way in which it became public: Chuck Stuart calling for help over a cellular telephone, the transcript of the conversation printed almost in its entirety; the fact that a film crew just happened to be on hand to record the dramatic scene in which the dying Carol and the badly wounded Chuck were removed from their car. Factor in the apparent randomness of the crime and the entirely believable scenario of a black drug user attacking a yuppie white couple deep in a bad section of town. This played on the fears not only of white Bostonians, but of white suburbanites everywhere, most of whom tend to look upon the inner city as a no-man's-land. It didn't have to be Boston; it could just as easily have been Detroit, Miami, Chicago, Atlanta, or Los Angeles.

But the story was pure soap opera. The murdered wife. The husband and the premature child struggling for survival. The child dying. The man writing a melodramatic letter that is read at her funeral. An outraged public. Police overreaction, compounded by the use of questionable stop-and-search tactics that infuriated the residents. Then came the announcement that there was a suspect, a black man with a history of senseless violence that included shooting a policeman. Witnesses came forth who were said to have confirmed the case against the black man, who was subsequently identified by the only surviving victim. Then, just when it appeared that the black man was going to be indicted, the case turned upside down.

That is powerful stuff indeed. Stronger than Sly Stallone. Stronger, even, than fiction. There were enough twists and turns in the case to make anyone dizzy, especially those who have tried to chronicle it.

Contributing to the confusion has been the fact that this is not just a crime story. It is a political story, too. And a story about the media; a story about race relations; about drugs; greed; friendship; psychology; morals; and family. Particularly family. Chuck Stuart came from such a tightly woven Irish family that two of his brothers would not turn him in even when they suspected that he had murdered his wife, a woman they had known for ten years, a woman they had accepted into the family and clasped to their bosom, a woman whose hospitality they had shared, whose meals they had enjoyed. It's staggering.

In the end, one of them cracked, probably not because he felt guilty about what had happened, but more likely because he knew that if he did not go to the authorities, his girlfriend would. And what about Matthew? How deeply is he really involved? The story Matthew has told seems improbable. It would require Chuck to have shot his wife and himself at one location and then, while badly wounded, dispose of the car keys, drive to a second location to meet Matthew, drive to a third location with Matthew following, and then drive still further while on the phone with the State Police. It is conceivable that it happened this way, but it seems more likely that when all the investigations are complete, investigators will not be buying the story, at least as it has been reported to date.

So what do we know? Precious little. We know that Carol Stuart is dead because she was shot in the head; that Chuck Stuart is dead as a result of drowning; and that seventeen-day-old Christopher Stuart is dead because he never had a chance. That's about it. We don't know what Matthew knows, or Michael or Jack McMahon. As far as Willie Bennett is concerned, we don't know why Flanagan has declined to rule him out as a suspect. Most of all, we don't know for sure if Chuck was guilty or if he committed suicide.

One of the most frustrating experiences in writing this story has been the appalling lack of official information. In most true-crime stories there is a paper trail to follow: court records, depositions, transcripts of interrogations, statements from investigators and prosecutors, police reports, public records, and on and on. In this case there has been nothing. At the first sign of heat, the police retreated like spoiled children into their treehouse, pulling the ladder up after them; then they parceled out bits and pieces of questionable material to those who knew the secret code, those who were their favorites. The district attorney did the same thing, except more is expected from him. He is an elected official, a man supposedly responsive and responsible to the public. He is one man, not an anonymous department. He is a lawyer, a public servant, a *career* protector of the people's rights. But Newman Flanagan apparently thinks that the less people know, the better off they are. The arrogance is mind-numbing.

Almost always in a criminal case *someone* is willing to talk. If not the prosecutor, then the lawyer for the defense. If not the police, then the defendant. In this case, everyone ran for cover. Everyone hired a lawyer; a small army of lawyers is currently, has been, or will be involved in this incredibly tangled case. When this was written, Willie Bennett had run through three lawyers. Matthew also had three, if you include the family friend he went to before he hired Perenyi. The Stuarts have a lawyer. The DeMaitis have a law firm. Janet Monteforte has a lawyer. Debbie Allen has a lawyer. Dereck Jackson has a lawyer. Jack McMahon had a lawyer. Eric Whitney has a lawyer. Alan Swanson had a lawyer. Only Chuck did not have a lawyer when he died (although he had one when he was in the hospital)—and not because he didn't try. His hospital lawyer had severed the relationship, and he apparently had not found a new one, although he called *somebody* from his hotel room. If all of these lawyers came into a courtroom at the same time, the jury would have to watch the proceedings over closed-circuit television from another floor. Providing this case ever gets to that stage. If it does come to trial, they might have to hold it in Fenway Park.

To me, it has been amazing to watch this process in action. To see doors that should be open locked, bolted, and chained with a German shepherd at the portal. Even the most basic information usually available in cases like this—autopsy reports for example—are deemed out of public reach. That is because Massachusetts considers itself a bastion of liberty, liberalism, and individual freedom. In this case individual freedom is working to the detriment of the group. But no one seems to be making much noise about it.

The very ones who are supposed to be watching out for the people have, in this case, turned their backs. The police have done it. The district attorney's office has done it. And the media, to a large extent, have done it as well. Reporters have fed happily on rumor, seemingly content to rush into print or on the air with the latest from the police locker room or the corner pub. And they think they have done a good job. The *Phoenix*'s media critic Mark Jurkowitz asked some of the principals at the two newspapers how they thought they had fared. A spokesperson from the *Herald* said the paper should get a B+ for its coverage; the editor at the *Globe* in charge of the Stuart case said, "From poor to excellent, I'd give it a good."

Coming from the *Globe*, that is particularly ironic. According to Jurkowitz, the *Globe* is perceived by the average Bostonian as an elitist publication demonstrably more interested in what happens in Pakistan than in what occurs on Park Street. This seems to be a remarkably accurate assessment, at least judging from the *Globe*'s coverage in the Stuart case. Although *The New York Times* can get away with a certain amount of snobbishness because of the general excellence of its coverage, the *Globe* cannot. It does not have the *Times*'s reputation for comprehensiveness, probity, or accuracy. It may be more reliable, over the long haul, than the *Herald*, but the *Globe* is no exemplar of meticulousness. Instead, judging by its coverage of the Stuart case, it has a certain propensity toward hysteria, complicated by questionable judgment, a tendency to sensationalize, and an eagerness to rush into print without regard to accuracy. It not only seemed satisfied to let its star columnist (a man who is paid to have strong, biased opinions) double as a reporter in the Stuart case, it was smug in its stance, seemingly encouraging the practice by giving front-page play both to his columns *and* to the news stories he coauthored.

One other thing is more than passing strange. Throughout most of the Stuart affair, the *Globe*'s editorial page has been unusually silent. There were no editorials, at least none that I saw, complaining about the withholding of information or the police department's derogation of responsibility in refusing to release precise, timely information regarding the progress of the investigation. Day after day the *Globe* chugged along attributing its Stuart information to anonymous sources, and the editorial page never thought it extraordinary.

Of course, that acceptance of glorified rumor has not been strictly a failing of the *Globe.* Seemingly, as far as the Boston media is concerned, Chuck shot Carol, then himself, then he jumped off the Tobin Bridge. End of story. I actually was surprised to read a *Globe* article on February 23 that referred to Chuck's death for the first time as an "apparent suicide." I'd very much like to know what was behind the change in wording. Did the newspapers' lawyers tell the city desk to insert the qualifier, maybe because of the potential battle in probate court in which Chuck's suicide or nonsuicide could be an issue?

But the Boston media were not alone. The television networks, the Associated Press, United Press International, *Time, Newsweek,* and, yes, *People* were part of the parade. Prior to the one example from the *Globe,* the only two newspapers that I have seen to use the word *alleged* when coupling it with *suicide* in talking about Chuck were *The New York Times* and the *Boston Phoenix.* And as far as the *Times* is concerned, the careful wording may be strictly a matter of habit. As Jurkowitz humorously pointed out in one of his media critiques, the *Times* reporters writing about Debbie Allen felt compelled to qualify their description of her beauty by noting that "friends say" she is an attractive woman.

Chuck may have, probably did, commit suicide. But so far it has not been proven. And the media is off base when it treats the incident as a matter of fact rather than speculation. A rumor around town had it that the district attorney's office had three witnesses who saw Chuck alone on the bridge, saw him climb over the rail, and saw him jump. If that is true, why has Flanagan not released these witnesses' names or at least announced officially that they exist? Why hasn't the *Globe* editorialized about *that*?

The FBI long ago completed its tests on the pistol that was recovered from the Pines River. Why have authorities not revealed the results of those tests? Was it the death weapon? Did it contain identifiable fingerprints (never mind *whose*)? How long had it been in the river? Whatever happened to Chuck's watch? to Carol's ruby ring? And when did Chuck put the car keys in the vacant lot?

How about the autopsy reports? How about the hospital records of two victims of violent death? Do they show that Carol was shot from the front seat or the backseat? Was the angle of entry such that Chuck could have shot himself? Did he have alcohol or drugs in his system when his body was recovered? Did his body show signs of violence other than what would have resulted from smacking into the surface of the river at 120 miles per hour?

The questions go on and on. Was Chuck involved in other scams? How much insurance *did* he have on his wife? When were the policies written and with whom? Why has the text of his alleged suicide note not been disclosed? Was it written in his hand? Why has his new car been locked away? What were the results of the DNA tests ordered because there was a question about whether he was actually the father of Carol's baby? Why did Matthew involve

Jack McMahon in disposing of Carol's belongings? And why would Jack McMahon get involved? Why was a third shot fired in the car that night? What was its trajectory? Was it from the same weapon? And what about Willie Bennett? Why does the DA say Bennett is not yet out of the picture? Is he merely trying to keep more records from the public, or does he have a more substantial reason for making that statement? Is Bennett's voice raspy? Why did Chuck give such a good description of him? Why did he point him out when he could just as easily have said none of them looked like his assailant? Why? Why? Why?

On the *People Are Talking* show Alan Dershowitz said that throughout the Stuart affair the people involved consistently revealed things they should not have (such as Perenyi and Clayman running on about their clients), while failing to reveal things they should have. He is absolutely correct. The list of things that have *not* been divulged in this case is infinitely longer than the list of things that have.

What about Debbie Allen? Was she dating Chuck? Was it threatening his marriage? Did Carol know about it? Could she have been a motive for the murder? What *are* the possible motives Chuck would have had for wanting to murder his wife? Here are some that have been suggested:

- He wanted the insurance money, either because he was greedy or because he wanted to use it to finance a restaurant.
- He wanted to stop Carol from going to the police to report that he was 1) dealing drugs, 2) running an insurance scam, 3) planning a big robbery at Kakas & Sons.

- He did not want to be a father.
- He did not want to be married anymore.
- He was angry because Carol was pregnant and would be quitting her job.
- There was another woman.

In an afternoon anyone with even a superficial knowledge of the circumstances and an active imagination can come up with half a dozen more. It makes for good gossip—but little knowledge.

There are too many unanswered questions for me to responsibly draw firm conclusions in saying unequivocally that Chuck shot Carol, that Chuck shot himself, that Matthew was an innocent pawn, that Willie Bennett's life has been ruined. Too many questions remain unanswered. Maybe the answers will come next week. Maybe next year. Maybe never. Maybe Flanagan will retire when *he* gets to be eighty years old and the Stuart documents will still be locked in his safe, perhaps to be revealed by the next crusading DA.

If the DA would tell what he knows. If the police would tell what they know. If the principals in the story, from Matthew and Michael Stuart to Mario DiMaiti, from Willie Bennett to Dereck Jackson, would tell their stories under oath and submit to cross-examination, then we might all have an approximate idea of what happened on the night of October 23 and why. In other words, if there is a trial.

Will there be a trial? Who knows? If I had to bet, I'd say no. Fear of a trial is the primary reason no one is talking. No one wants to say too much, because then a trial might be a necessity. If the case can be allowed to die as it is, it is all wrapped up nicely and neatly. If no one else knows what *they* know and what *they* don't know, no one can accuse *them* of covering things up.

But it is not only the prosecutors and the police who do not want to talk. If there is a trial, or even a public hearing, there is no way the testimony could be restricted to matters applying only to a criminal case. Politics would come oozing out of every seam and crack. And nobody involved wants that. The DA doesn't want to be accused of incompetence. Neither do the police. Mayor Flynn doesn't want to have to answer allegations of racism. Black leaders do not want to have to face accusations that they overreacted to the arrest of Willie Bennett. Willie Bennett does not want to talk in public, period; he doesn't want anyone to hear his voice. Michael Stuart doesn't want to declaim publicly about how he lived with himself for months without telling the world that his brother may have been a wife killer. Neither does Matthew, who already has admitted *some* role. Journalists don't want to have to admit they may have been snookered a second time. The *Globe*, watching its reputation, doesn't want to admit how sloppy its coverage was. The *Herald* probably doesn't care. One thing about being a Murdoch tabloid is that no one expects a lot.

To go back to the beginning: Did Chuck do it? If I were sitting on a jury and the only evidence I had heard is what has been revealed so far, I would feel compelled to vote for acquittal. After all, our system of jurisprudence requires that a man be proved guilty beyond a reasonable doubt. I do not necessarily believe Chuck Stuart is innocent—but at this writing he has not been proved guilty of the crime of which he is accused.

Ken Englade

CHRONOLOGY

1989

September —Chuck Stuart approaches Michael and asks him if he knows someone who would be willing to commit a murder.

October —Chuck asks an old friend, David MacLean, if he would kill his wife, Carol.

October —Rebuffed by both his brother Michael and his friend, Chuck asks another brother, Matthew, to help him with a scheme to defraud an insurance company. Matthew agrees.

October 13 —Chuck and Carol Stuart celebrate their fourth wedding anniversary by spending a weekend at an inn in Connecticut.

October 23 —A man obviously in pain calls state police on his car telephone and says he and his wife have been shot by a gunman and are in need of assistance. By listening to the sirens of searching police cars, rescue units zero in on the car, which is pulled to the side of the road in one of Boston's worst inner-city neighborhoods. Inside the vehicle is a gravely wounded Chuck Stuart and his dying wife, Carol. They are rushed to separate hospitals, but the pregnant Carol undergoes an immediate cesarean section. Her baby, a boy whom the family names Christopher, is not expected to live. Chuck undergoes abdominal surgery and is placed in intensive care.

October 24   —Carol dies. Chuck describes the alleged assailant to police as a black man with a patchy beard and a raspy voice.

October 26   —Michael Stuart learns from his brother Matthew that their other brother, Chuck, was involved in the shooting of his wife. They say nothing to anyone else.

October 28   —Funeral services are held for Carol. Some eight hundred people attend, including the governor, the mayor, the police commissioner, and the city's highest-ranking Roman Catholic prelate.

October 29 or 30 —Matthew leaves Boston for California. Stays away for six weeks.

November 7   —A black man named Alan Swanson surfaces as the first serious suspect. The case against him is very weak, and he eventually is released.

November 9   —Baby Christopher Stuart dies at Boston City Hospital. Age, seventeen days.

November 11   —A black man with a long criminal record and a history of violence is arrested.
His name is William "Willie" Bennett. He is
charged with armed robbery, but police department leaks say he is the main suspect in the Stuart
shooting.

November 15   —A grand jury begins an investigation of the shooting with the focus on Bennett.

November 21   —A black teenager named Dereck Jackson tells the grand jury that he heard
Bennett confess to shooting the Stuarts. Soon afterward he recants his testimony, saying police intimidated him into implicating Bennett. He is followed
by another black teenager who also had testified
against Bennett.

November 23   —Bennett is ordered held on
$50,000 bail for a video store holdup.

December 5   —Chuck Stuart is released from
Boston City Hospital. Almost immediately he col-
lects $82,000 on a policy his wife had taken out
through the firm where she worked. Soon afterward he applies to collect on a separate policy of
$100,000.

December 24   —Matthew Stuart's girlfriend,
Janet Monteforte, goes to a lawyer and tells him
that Matthew and his brother Chuck were involved
in the incident.

December 28   —Chuck views a police lineup,
singles out Bennett as the man who looks "most
like" his assailant.

December 29   —Bennett is charged with an additional robbery but still not with the murder of Carol and Christopher Stuart.

1990

January 1   —Michael, Matthew, and Janet tell brother Mark and half sister Shelly that Chuck was directly involved in Carol's shooting. Matthew says he has decided to go to authorities on January 3.

January 3   —Using a $10,000 certified check, which was part of his insurance money, and the trade-in value of the 1987 Toyota Cressida he was driving the night of the shooting, Chuck buys a new Nissan Maxima for $22,277.

          Late in the day, Matthew and his friend, John "Jack" McMahon go to prosecutors.

          Between 9:00 and 10:00 P.M., Chuck checks into a hotel. Leaves a wake-up call for 4:30 A.M. Makes one outside phone call to a local number. Hotel officials say since it was a local call there was no record of the number in its automatic equipment.

January 4   —About 2:00 A.M. Chuck gets restless and goes across the street to an all-night convenience store to buy a soda and a snack.

          7:00 A.M. His two-day-old car is found on the Tobin Bridge. On the seat is a note in which Chuck allegedly says he cannot stand the allegations being made against him. He does *not* confess to the murders.

          12:30 P.M. Chuck's body is recovered from the Mystic River.

          Late that day, a news release

from the district attorney's office says that Willie
Bennett is no longer a suspect in the Stuart shootings.

The city's black leaders an-
nounce their outrage at the way Willie Bennett and
the residents of Mission Hill were treated by police.
Some demand an apology from Mayor Flynn; others demand his resignation.

January 6   —Chuck is buried with services
at the Immaculate Conception Church in Revere.
No politicians attend.

January 10   —The DA's office announces that
a new grand jury will be convened to study the
Stuart case.

January 12   —The new grand jury begins taking testimony in the Stuart case. It recesses until
January 31.

January 26   —Carol's parents, Giusto and
Evelyn DiMaiti, announce the creation of a special
foundation in their daughter's name to provide
scholarships to needy students from Mission Hill.
Donations quickly top the $250,000 mark.

January 31   —An assistant in the district attorney's office files a document in a related case
indicating that Willie Bennett is not totally out of
the picture as a possible suspect in the Stuart
shooting.

Grand jury takes more testimony. Recesses until February 2.

February 2   —More testimony before the
grand jury. The group recesses until February 23.

February 23   —Grand jury meets again. Recesses for the weekend.

February 26   —The grand jury is expected to reconvene.

STOP PRESS

As this book was going to press, a development occurred that is worth noting:

- The U.S. attorney in Boston, Wayne Budd, ordered FBI agents to begin a preliminary inquiry into charges that Boston police had coerced witnesses to implicate Willie Bennett in the Stuart shooting. The purpose of the probe is to determine if a more extensive investigation is warranted. Police Commissioner Francis Roache called the action a "very positive step" and said his department would cooperate.

Lisa Steinberg—six years old and defenseless, she was the brutalized victim of a couple's descent into delusion and violence.

Joel Steinberg—cruel and controlling, he ruled his family with intimidation and a deadly iron fist.

Hedda Nussbaum—beaten and brainwashed, did her loyalty to Joel keep her from saving Lisa—or was there a more disturbing reason?

Never before has a trial been so shocking, nor testimony so riveting. Here for the first time is the entire heart-rending story of an outwardly normal family living in the shadow of violence and fear, and the illegally adopted, innocent girl whose life was the price of affection. Retold in the framework of the sensational trial, it is a sad and gripping tale that stabs at the heart's tenderest core.

LISA, HEDDA & JOEL
The Steinberg Murder Case

Documented with 8 pages of gripping photographs

WANTED

True Crime From St. Martin's Paperbacks!